PRAISE FOR LEADERSHIP BEYOND GENDER

Leadership Beyond Gender challenges long held beliefs, assumptions and stereotypes about gender and leadership. Dr. Ray offers scientifically based theories supported by real life experience, wisdom and intellect. Experienced leaders, new leaders and aspiring leaders will greatly benefit from the insights and information shared by Dr. Ray. *Leadership Beyond Gender* offers proof that when our clear intentions drive our attention transformation will happen."

Connie L. Lindsey
Executive Vice President-Northern Trust Company
National President, Girl Scouts of the USA

Leadership Beyond Gender will become an instant classic among the leadership literature. Dr. Ray brings the clarity of John Kotter's change strategy; the insight of Daniel Goleman's Emotional Intelligence framework; and the practical wisdom of Marshall Goldsmith to a field that will transform how leaders think...and act. Her insights satisfy both the yearnings of the heart and the curiosity of the intellect and provide a clear pathway for anyone committed to being more effective. It is rare that you CAN tell a book from its cover—in this case, the promise of greater vision delivers!

Aleen Bayard
Adjunct faculty, Northwestern University
Principal MarketZing

Leadership Beyond Gender broadens the reader's awareness of self and others. It is the next step to being a more effective leader.

Charles Brummell
President and CEO
Lupus Foundation of America, Illinois Chapter

D1253244

LEADERSHIP
BEYOND GENDER

Transcend Limiting Mindsets to
Become a More Engaging Leader

Valencia Ray, M.D.

LEADERSHIP BEYOND GENDER
Transcend Limiting Mindsets to
Become a More Engaging Leader

Valencia Ray, M.D.
Empower Up Publishing

Published by Empower Up Publishing, Naperville, Illinois
Copyright ©2013 Valencia Ray, M.D.
All rights reserved.

Library of Congress Control Number: 2013950996
ISBN: 978-0-9823680-2-2

This book is not designed to and does not provide medical advice, professional diagnoses, opinions, treatment or services to the reader. It provides general information for educational purposes only and is not a substitute for medical or professional care. The author is not liable or responsible for any use of information in this book in lieu of prompt consultation with a physician or other healthcare professional.

Dedication

This book is dedicated to my husband Darrell Jackson, whom I admire and who leads with mind and heart by example.

CONTENTS

Everyone thinks of changing the world,
but no one thinks of changing himself.

— Leo Tolstoy

We are under tremendous pressure to learn new, more productive behaviors and skills, and to find new ways to adapt to the demands of our times. We are searching for new answers, but is there a blind spot that is constricting our vision for the future of leadership development?

Understand the roots of inauthenticity and how our brain creates "self-fulfilling prophecy." Achieving a leadership advantage in the workplace requires us to re-write our story so we can generate new and much better outcomes.

Discover what it means to "optimally operate" your brain's inner technology and learn how to begin to expand the vision in your "Mind's Eye." Understand "Neuroscience 101" basics and how these apply to you as a leader.

Understand how the "Battle of the Sexes" correlates with the battle between our left-brain and right-brain hemispheres, which represent mind and heart respectively. Learn how gender perception has literally impacted how our brain wires stereotypical behaviors and about the scientific evidence demonstrating this perception can be changed to meet leadership development needs.

ACKNOWLEDGEMENTS

To my past loyal employees and patients who taught me over a decade ago the power and value of collaborative leadership culture, purpose-driven service and heart-felt values to ignite positive transformation that can improve the quality of life for all who are engaging in workplace relationships—as well as the business financial bottom line.

Last but not least, special thanks to my brilliant colleagues and friends whose feedback and support has been invaluable and greatly appreciated.

There are a thousand hacking at the branches of evil
to one who is striking at the root.

— Henry David Thoreau

DOES LEADERSHIP REALLY HAVE A GENDER?

The definitive answer to this question is ***no!*** Many people incorrectly believe that leadership style is determined biologically by one's gender, as exemplified by business conversations in the media on "Male Leadership versus Female Leadership" comparisons. This gender focus powerfully illustrates our lack of understanding about how our brains can create the way that we view ourselves and our lives and how our brains can shape the way we operate in the world as men and women. This book is not another book about gender issues *per se*. It is written for men and women and addresses a new way of dealing with change and the leadership demands facing both genders. I use gender as it relates to leadership in order to illustrate how we have unwittingly trained our brains in ways that limit our true potential as leaders and keep us stuck in ineffective and unproductive patterns. The principles in this book can be applied to our blind spots as they relate to cultural stereotyping and other diverse workforce issues, including performance on every level. This lack of "brain-awareness" also literally impacts our own ability to be successful and fulfilled in all areas of our lives. I use gender and leadership as the context for illustrating how our mindsets can get stuck—regardless of gender. Gender stereotyping, for example, is applicable to men who stereotype other men and women who unconsciously stereotype other women as well. Brain-based stereotyping is an equal opportunity phenomenon.

As leaders, we look everywhere for ways to make a greater impact, but as a whole, we often fail—despite all of our training, experiences, and intellect. If you are reading this book, there's a good chance that you have come across articles in online business magazines and leadership blogs, or have listened to panel discussions sponsored by well-respected universities that hotly debate leadership attributes based upon gender. Even if you have not been exposed to much of the discourse regarding this topic, you may be curious about it since the "hot topic" of gender is often presented as one of the dominant reasons we cannot rise to the occasion. While the gender argument regarding "Male Leadership" versus "Female Leadership" can *point* us to the root of our lack of success, however, we need to seriously consider that there is a deeper question that is really *at the root* of our dilemma.

Quite simply, the gender argument is a symptom; not a solution. It is a symptom of our lack of understanding of how our brains can literally *create the way* that we see ourselves and others. How we wire our brain literally impacts our performance in all areas. This brain-created process is subjective and changeable—and most people are totally unaware of how they direct their brains in self-limiting, ineffective ways at the office and at home. The *way that we focus* our brains can determine whether or not we are effective in achieving our business and personal goals. In that context, gender stereotyping can be traced to our lack of self-awareness of how to *"optimally operate"* our amazing brains. This ultimately affects organizational effectiveness. Thanks to new discoveries in neuroscience, we can begin to accelerate personal development and self-awareness in a way that supports the individual and the organization in creating more productive and effective behaviors and outcomes.

As we begin, there is an important question to ask ourselves. Are we struggling in the area of leadership because we are male or female, or is there something deeper at the root of what is holding us back? **Innovation is about thinking differently.** By focusing only on stereotypical gender arguments, we are being distracted from the real issues of how to effectively adapt and lead change in a rapidly evolving world. More importantly, we ignore the innovative ideas presented by brain research.

TWO ISSUES THAT ARE THE FOCUS OF THIS BOOK

If we as leaders are to effectively respond to 21st century challenges, I believe the following issues are central to our exploration of leadership and its requisite transformation.

Where we currently are:

1. Does sex determine our leadership ability? In fact, what is the difference between "gender" and "biological sex," and how does this impact us as leaders?

While the gender debate is not the source of our leadership ineffectiveness, it is an important issue for me to address in this book because it reveals one of the most common symptoms that impedes leadership development progress. *The gender debate exposes how we have unwittingly wired our brain to be inflexible and cling to old ways of thinking, even in the face of empirical and scientific, factual progress.* The actual source of our leadership ineffectiveness is more related to *how* we have wired our brain to see the world perceptually. Our "Mind's Eye" needs a new vision.

Where do we go from here?

2. Can we retrain our brains so that we can become more effective leaders, regardless of gender?

In order to become more effective leaders, regardless of gender, there is a need to ask new and better questions, given the timely and enlightening brain research that demonstrates that our brain is able to rewire itself far beyond what we ever imagined possible. In effect, we can change behavior. When we ask new and better questions, our brains will seek and find new and better solutions. Addressing these two questions is therefore a primary focus of this book.

THE GENESIS OF THIS BOOK

This book itself is born out of my lived experience with the subject matter discussed in this book. Its content is not theory for me because I have lived through the impact my mindset shift has had upon me and upon my business and its employees. My personal study and life experiences have led me to integrate my formal training in neuroscience into my understanding of the mind. I am passionate about uncovering the blind spots that have hindered my performance, either personally or professionally. I sold my medical eye surgery practice so I could take my life purpose of restoring vision to a whole new level, this time, focusing on the Mind's Eye. This experiential understanding of weaving together into a whole the spiritual, emotional, mental, and physical parts of myself has made and continues to make me a more effective and happier human being. There has never been a better opportunity to embrace change than living in the world as it exists today. There are ample reasons for us to strive to develop our true potential. Using neuroscience (brain science) to open a logical and heartfelt conversation on how to do this is a very important piece of solving the dilemmas we are facing in our rapidly changing world. Read on to begin learning ways to transcend your limiting beliefs so you can become a more engaging leader—regardless of your gender.

HOW TO GET THE MOST FROM THIS BOOK

Engaging this book with an open-mind is very important. Intention matters. Before now, as professionals and entrepreneurs, we have focused much of our learning on tactical skills while dismissing the importance of self-knowledge and self-management. Since this is a new paradigm, it's important that I lay a foundation and set the context for where we are and how we arrived,—in addition to providing new findings in a way that is not "sciency." You will need this information to get where you want to go. In an effort to do this well, I will avoid technical terms as much as possible and instead use metaphors, anecdotes, and business contexts while sharing the science. Begin by seeing this as an adventure—and not simply "more to learn."

In part I of this book, I will share some background history and explore how we arrived at our current mindset dilemma regarding gender behavior. I also will share some foundational cognitive neuroscience research to support my argument that we are not "hard-wired" for gender behavior. I will share some basic information on the science behind how we unwittingly create identity stereotypes for ourselves and for others and what guides the wiring of our brains. This information is important so that you can become conscious of how you are currently "wiring" your own brain. In part II I will provide a short self-evaluation that will enable you to begin to put brain hemisphere-based behaviors into context. I will share real-life case studies of how left and right-brain behaviors are manifest, compared to how a more collaborative integration of our brain hemispheres would theoretically manifest. I will also share practical tools and exercises that will help you shape your own mind for better leadership skill development and overall well-being.

Each chapter will end in a short list of "Key Points," "Reflect: Inquiring Mind" questions, and "Envision Possibilities" considerations. It will help you to understand and digest this new material if you make time to pause and reflect instead of simply reading through to the end in order to "get the answers." In fact, it is a good idea to have a journal notebook available as you are reading so you can make notes of "aha" moments and insights.

Engaging mind with heart is the winning combination needed to flourish in business and in life in the 21st century. Integration of your whole brain, your whole self, transcends so-called gender limitations. The old competitive "survival of the fittest" paradigm will no longer work in this new environment. The leader who can adapt to and lead change in a positive direction is the one who will thrive. Instead of wasting time arguing gender difference, *the focus must be on creating a more sustainable organizational model and environment as well as more fulfilling and meaningful lives for others and ourselves.* This is the path to "sustainable engagement."

Changing the behavior of people is the most important
challenge for businesses trying to compete in a turbulent world.

— John Kotter, Harvard Business School

Leaders who embrace continuous, life-long learning will pave the way for the collaborative effort needed to reach the next higher evolution of growth for humankind. Will you join us?

PART 1:
THE ROOTS OF
INAUTHENTICITY

Everyone thinks of changing the world,
but no one thinks of changing himself

— Leo Tolstoy

CHAPTER ONE

AN OPPORTUNITY FOR LEADERSHIP DEVELOPMENT

You never let a serious crisis go to waste.
And what I mean by that it's an opportunity to do things
you think you could not do before.

— Rahm Emanuel, Mayor of Chicago

I believe one reason we are having the perennial debate around gender is because, as leaders, we are struggling to make an impact. However, many of us still feel we are making insufficient progress due to things beyond our control. We are faced with unprecedented challenges in our institutions overall as well as challenges in our environments. We are under tremendous pressure to learn new, more productive behaviors and skills, and to find new ways to adapt to the demands of our times. Employee disengagement is at an all-time high. This is exacerbated by a four-generation workplace with conflicting values and styles of leadership and communication. Time is of the essence and it is important for us to search for innovative answers by asking relevant and new, powerful questions that can help us to adapt to these changes. Our gifts, skills, and abilities may have been good enough in the past, but now they are no longer getting the job done effectively. We are being required to learn more productive behaviors that can inspire others to successful action and help us to navigate, with much greater ease, the changes we are facing daily on many levels. We are searching for new answers, but is there a blind spot that is constricting our vision for the future of leadership development?

As you will learn in this book, focusing on the gender argument can give us a window through which to look for opportunities to grow as leaders, both personally and professionally. Using this context of gender can help illustrate the forces that form our attitudes, beliefs, and behaviors so that we can begin to learn how to purposely create more authentic choices that work for our own development and for the good of the whole organization. Historically, the arguments for gender differences are deeply rooted in cultural and social norms. However, we now have new brain research demonstrating that cognitive behavior is not rooted in biology but instead is greatly influenced by experience and environment—far more than previously recognized. It is very important for us to examine and understand the role that our brain perceptions play in forming assumptions that lead to self-fulfilling prophecies in our behavior—*literally*. Lack of awareness of this concept is what is at the root of our leadership challenge. Increasing our self-awareness and the application of new brain research *will help us to take leadership beyond gender arguments*. The conversations we need to have should examine how we are able to retrain our brains so that we can be more effective and engaging leaders, regardless of gender.

GETTING TO THE ROOT OF THE MATTER

From brain research and from my own personal journey, I know that "*how*" we direct our attention powerfully impacts both our performance and "who we think we are" at a physiologic, bodily level. It is time to go deeper to uncover the roots of our leadership behavior instead of staying at the surface by focusing only on, (to use Thoreau's image from the introduction), "the branches." Yes, we are smart and we are smart enough to learn how to embrace continuous learning. It is only perception that taints leadership development with the idea that personal growth means we are "fixing" ourselves. We are simply expanding our self-awareness so as to be able to skillfully meet the current challenges before us. We need not only to stay abreast of the latest tactile skills, but we also need to stay current regarding the innovations that teach us how to be more engaging, creative, and higher performing leaders—from the inside out.

Focusing on gender as the reason for one's behavior and leadership performance is like hacking at the branches. Actually, this focus on gender is creating a "blind spot," from a brain standpoint, that hinders us from looking for new solutions. And this focus will not help us get to the root cause of our ineffectiveness. Through self-awareness and by better understanding how to *"optimally operate"* our whole brain, we are able to change our brain right down to its physical structure and function in a way that creates changes in perception and, subsequently, behavior. The following is a simple example of how perceptions that form blind spots work. Imagine you are at an offsite leadership training experience. Of the following two questions, which one would you be willing and comfortable raising your hand to answer if asked?

1. How many of you need to fix yourselves so that you can reach more of your true potential?

2. How many of you need to learn and grow in order to reach more of your true potential?

Can you feel the difference between these two questions? The first question implies (gives the perception) that you are defective or "broken." This would naturally trigger a self-defensive, flight/fight/freeze response in the brain, which is not a good response if one desires cooperation from employees with learning and development. This kind of question serves to illustrate why people so commonly resist admitting that they need to change their behaviors. We have a perception that it is "bad" to admit our need for behavioral change, so it becomes a self-fulfilling prophecy—we feel bad about it! Research has shown that we can literally, physiologically, change the meaning that we assign to situations and circumstances, including how we perceive growth and development in the workplace. Just imagine how much easier behavioral change would be if there was much less resistance and it was embraced. According to Daniel Pink's research in his book *Drive,* what sustainably motivates people to higher levels of performance are intrinsic factors such as autonomy, self-mastery, and purpose. An increasing number of people really do desire to actualize more of their true potential; they just need to learn how to change the way they perceive "behavioral change."

The ability of the brain to change itself and its perceptions is known as "neuroplasticity," and this capacity for change is far greater than scientists ever imagined. After all, innovation means "change" and, if we are to adapt with greater ease, we need to better understand how to more effectively operate the "inner technology" of our own brain. A new research study titled *Global Talent 2012* and referred to in Towers and Watson's *Global Workforce 2012* report cites "mental and interpersonal agility" as two competencies that will be in high demand within the next 5–10 years. Neuroscience, which is research that involves the brain and nervous system, has arrived in the nick of time to help us to better understand ourselves so that we can not only improve our performance, but also create healthier relationships and lifestyles. This translates to an ability to create new solutions, products, and improved customer service. These positive changes would naturally lead to higher levels of leadership skill and to healthier and more change-ready organizational cultures.

> *The important thing is to never stop questioning.*
> — Albert Einstein

We are being challenged to deal with traditional leadership behavior and styles that need to evolve because these impact and limit the leadership skills of both men and women. While the question of gender and leadership is a "hot debate" and a very interesting one, is this the question on which we really need to focus?

NEW QUESTIONS FOR A NEW DIRECTION

As leaders, we are being asked to move forward with more adaptability, clarity, resilience, and wisdom and to lead our organizational teams in the face of massive change. Given the situations with which we are confronted, more relevant questions would be:

- *How can we as leaders, both male and female, best accomplish this in light of the most recent findings on brain plasticity and behavior?*

- *How do we adapt and evolve our leadership styles in order to rise to the occasion?*

- *Can we all tap more of our true potential and rise to meet these challenges by learning how to better optimize our whole brain, regardless of gender?*

Doug Conant, the former CEO of Campbell Soup Company and the person who led the remarkable turnaround of the company, said in a *Harvard Business Review* blog podcast interview dated October 13, 2011:

> *Leadership is a nuanced craft and I think when times change you have to evolve your leadership style.*

To develop your unique authentic way of "being" as a leader, you must first develop your "intrapersonal" relationship—your relationship with yourself. Our organizations cannot be efficiently run by a one-size-fits-all leadership style and, certainly, categorizing people based on gender stereotypes is neither wise nor productive, especially in a rapidly changing environment. The challenge is to "know thyself" and to break free of limiting beliefs in an enlightened way before you can lead people in an enlightened way.

Neuroplasticity of the brain allows us to change our leadership styles and to expand our minds on a personal level. What we thought of as "hard-wired behaviors" or limitations as men and women are not true and this is good news! In this book, I am going to talk about how we can transcend stereotypes and their limitations by asking new and different questions, and by better understanding how we can apply the revolutionary information telling us that we really can "retrain our brain" for more effective and efficient behavioral choices. Science substantiates that we are not victims of our brain, genes, or gender.

I submit that arguing over gender differences in leadership styles, particularly given objective research that apparently is being ignored, is not an effective use of our precious intellectual resources and time. Science tells us that we can transcend gender stereotypes and that behaviors that no longer serve us can be changed. Debating gender superiority is a distraction and does not serve the need of the hour—to develop 21st century leaders who are able to lead change first within their selves and then to inspire others to evolve, thereby creating organizational cultures that can innovate and grow to meet the challenges of the ever-changing global marketplace.

CREATING A NEW BUSINESS REALITY

Back in 2002, when I began to bring what I had learned about organizational change to my office, my goal was to help my employees grow personally because I realized that this was the key to their professional growth as well. We had been experiencing team dysfunction such as absenteeism, implicit communication challenges, and suboptimal customer service at the reception desk. I wanted employees to enjoy coming to work and I wanted to positively change the atmosphere (culture). I also had the goal of providing outstanding customer service to my patients/clients. By focusing on these three priorities, the service delivery and culture evolved rapidly. I became genuinely interested in my employees' personal and professional development. I helped them to engage their hearts by bringing values, purpose, and mission into the conversation. We explicitly addressed emotional intelligence and how it impacted customer service. I trained them to be able to integrate their job functions, which broke down the silo mentality. The change in the work environment was palpable. Our clients often commented on how efficient, effective, and pleasant our office had become. Advertising and marketing took care of themselves via word of mouth from our avidly happy and satisfied clients and referring physicians. Even though I didn't even have a website, I had more than enough clients to serve. I had successfully created my ideal medical business based on my current personal and professional needs, and I knew I was fulfilling my purpose as I envisioned it at the time.

THE RESULTS OF RETRAINING OUR BRAINS

Focusing on personal development, customer service, and culture is what transformed my business and created a win-win-win for my employees, the clients, and me. We even won the community service award for Outstanding Service in 2004, only two years after implementing the changes in my office.

What would be possible for you and your organization if you were to experience even a few of the following shifts and results I experienced while leading my medical practice?

- Increased employee ownership, alignment, and loyalty

- Decreased absenteeism and happy team members

- Improved collaborative leadership and team building skills

- Increased personal confidence in yourself and in your team members

- Greater productivity due to more individual autonomy, meaning, and less stress

- Greater clarity in strategic visioning and implementation

- Accessing core values from a place in the "heart" which increases commitment

- Access to innovation and diversity of thought

- A workplace environment that supports personal development

- Improved customer service and accountability

- Marked decrease in mistrust and fear of conflict

- Increased revenues due to greater efficiency and effective relationship practices

- A culture that embraces change and can adapt quickly to an ever-changing environment

I experienced all of these results firsthand when, as a practicing eye surgeon, I transformed *myself, which led to the transformation of my medical practice.* This personal and organizational transformation moved me to sell my medical practice so that I could fully dedicate myself to helping entrepreneurs and corporate leaders/professionals to eliminate what I call, "cataracts of the mind and heart" that block them from seeing and realizing their true potential in business and life. These "blind spots" also cloud one's sense of purpose and passion, and they hinder overall organizational culture and effectiveness.

In a practical real-life way, I have been able to blend my formal education in neuroscience as a medical eye surgeon with my experience of leading a successful business in a way that speaks to the changes that leaders are facing. From my own experience and from working with leaders at all levels, I know that all of the results I detailed are possible when you consciously engage both sides of your brain, and lead with intellect **and** heart! Research supports the power of the heart—the source of courage, meaning, faith, and inspiration—to drive change and to stimulate commitment to an idea or value. I have sold my medical practice now in order to help bring my experience to a broader context in my new role as a keynote speaker, corporate consultant, and executive coach. I desire to help others find clarity for their own lives. Expanding vision has its benefits.

THE BLIND SPOT OF STEREOTYPE; THE BENEFITS OF VISION

Will not a tiny speck very close to our vision blot out the glory of the world, and leave only a margin by which we see the blot?

— George Eliot, *Middlemarch*

Expanding your vision will require having a foundation of new insights. In order for you to explore "what you don't know that you don't know," I will need to guide you through some basic information about your brain. You will not be able to logically understand the new solutions I offer if you do not have a science-based context for the tools and exercises. Research shows that engaging with awareness your "logical brain," which is the left side of your brain, can reduce resistance to learning new information because this takes it out of the "airy-fairy" realm for many people. This helps you to maintain an open-mind. This is not another patchwork approach; this is about learning how to develop your own Art and Science of NeuroReInvention® in order to become a more effective, engaging leader. This is a more holistic approach. Both brain hemispheres contribute to behavior, creativity and innovation but in different ways. Art is more colorful and less predictable and is represented by our right-brain. Science is more linear and likes predictability, as represented by our left-brain. If we desire to be the most effective we can be, we need to bring these two worlds within ourselves back together again. This is the secret to sustainable dynamic leadership, performance, and well-being. The data is in; we can rewire our brains for sustained improved performance. Of course, it goes without saying that you must desire to do so.

What stereotyping **(be it gender, age, or culture)** and holding oneself and others "in boxes" tends to do is to hold people—and organizations—hostage to the "fight, flight, or freeze" levels of our brain. I call these areas of our brain our "Survival Brain." This term describes the brain function that holds old ways of being and thinking that keep people stuck in role-playing and can unconsciously provoke discomfort when others don't "act" as expected. We become "hijacked" before we can make the choices that could move our teams and organizations forward. Instead, we continue to do the same things in the same way, all the while expecting different results. This doesn't work.

In order to break through these blind spots and act in the present moment, we need to learn how to connect with the most highly evolved area of our brain. I call this area of our brain our "Thrival Brain." It is formally known as the neo-cortex. When we understand how to "optimally operate" our brain and intentionally access more of our Thrival Brain with purpose, we can quiet the Survival Brain and better connect emotionally with our teams because we have greater clarity, confidence, peace of mind, and have elevated our decision making and strategies. We can access our inner genius and stimulate more innovation. We adapt to change easier and act with more resilience. We can change our office climate and create healthier, more productive cultures that are sustainable over the long-term. Neuroscience is a potent path to helping us reach these goals much faster than we otherwise would have been able to do.

If you have highly developed tactical skill, yet realize that you need to hone your people-skill, problem-solving, and creative ability, this book deals with the root of how to get there. Getting to know yourself better and tapping into the "Authentic Leader Within" can free you from robotic, ineffective thinking and behaviors that no longer work.

WHAT ARE EXAMPLES OF BLIND SPOTS?

"Blind spot" is a medical term used by all eye surgeons (ophthalmologists). We all have a small blind spot in our healthy eyes that is formed by the optic nerve fibers exiting the retina en route to the brain. In fact, the optic nerve can be thought of as an extension of the brain. In diseases such as glaucoma, a disease that causes progressive blindness, people initially do not even realize they are developing blind spots until they have lost much of their vision. It is likely that they could have prevented future hardship if only they had acted earlier. This is a metaphor for what can happen to leaders in business. In business, leaders can develop blind spots of the "mind's eye" that keep them from seeing and taking advantage of the situation right before their eyes. They lack "inner-sight" or clear mind sight and miss new ideas that could lead to innovation and new opportunities.

As leaders, we commonly have a few blind spots that progress with time because of our lack of self-awareness. If we do not understand how our brain forms perception, that is, "*how* we see the world," we can continue to run our organizations in a way that leads to progressive loss of vision and future sustainable success. History is replete with corporate giants that once were household names but have now disappeared from the landscape simply due to being unaware of how to change course in a way that is adaptable and serves the current environmental demand. Blockbuster is a recent example of this type of corporate inflexibility that led to its own demise. Because Blockbuster executives did not keep their

Mind's Eye open to see new opportunities, they were blinded to the obvious. Blockbuster, founded in 1985, was the market leader in DVD home movie rental. Yet they let a start-up like Netflix beat them in their own space. Netflix, while it didn't have the financial capital, made use of the postal service and the Internet, while Blockbuster continued to focus on its old business model—it was time to change. Netflix brought innovation to Blockbuster's business model. Change had come, like it or not. Unfortunately, Blockbuster's leadership kept doing things the same old way—an example of the mental rigidity that can limit the true potential of a company. Blockbuster's founder, David Cook, who sold the company in 1987, is quoted in an October 17, 2010 *Time Magazine* article. "It didn't have to be this way," he says. "They let technology eat them up." Cook went on to form two successful technology companies.

The gender argument, as it relates to leadership competency, is a parallel to the type of blind spot that Blockbuster demonstrated. It illustrates how human beings can become stuck in paradigms that no longer serve the whole in an effective, productive manner and, in fact, are potentially destructive to the future of the organization. While we can deny the facts before our eyes, change can still run us over, catching us like deer in the headlights. Fortunately, if we so choose, we can evolve our thinking to be adaptable to the needs of our current world, thus leading to greater personal and professional success.

EXPANDING OUR VISION

One of my goals for this book is to allow both men and women to understand how stereotyping affects both genders. This is not just a "female problem." Male leadership development is also hindered by old stereotyping of how "real men" are *supposed* (stereotyping) to be. Effective 21st century leadership requires mental and emotional flexibility on many levels.

Before moving forward, I will provide a working definition of what I mean by "stereotype." I like the definition offered by University of California Davis psychologist, Jeffery Sherman, PhD. According to Dr. Sherman, stereotypes are defined as "Knowledge or expectations about members of a social group. Stereotypes are not only descriptive, but they are also *'prescriptive,'* that is, we think that members **should** behave in these ways." With this definition in mind, what are some obvious arguments that offer a gender stereotype? The following is an example of just one such discussion I have encountered.

A panel of academic researchers at UC Davis Graduate School of Management hosted a discussion entitled, "Empowering Women to Fill a Seat at the Table." Dr. Jeffery Sherman, who was on the panel, reported that from surveyed information, women and men leaders where perceived differently based on gender and gender alone. He reported that women were judged more poorly, even when their performance was the same as that of male leaders. The research findings according to Dr. Sherman, revealed a stereotype of women as being "warm but incompetent…not confident." If the assessment was done in a gender-blind way, there would be no differentiation between men and women.

On the flip side, if a woman a tries to behave in the stereotypical "macho" male way or exhibits "typical" CEO behavior—again, a stereotype not necessarily authentic to the actual person involved—she is often ostracized and punished by both men and women. Women are often disliked if they are "assertive," and are often considered "aggressive" if they do not stick with their assigned stereotypically docile behavior. They are then sometimes called unpleasant names if they step outside of their prescribed box. Men need not deal with this type of response to assertive behavior in general.

Of course, men as well have their own set of challenges, albeit different, regarding stereotypes. The old traditional image of the "alpha male," an aggressive go-getter who puts work before self, family, and other personal values really is not an accurate view for many modern-day men. In 2008, the Families and Work Institute found that 60% of men in dual-earner couples reported work-family conflict; this was up from 35% in 1977. Additionally, the traditional leadership style that is totally top-down and not inclusive of the insights from others who have a lower rank in the hierarchical structure tends to disengage people. This style is often referred to as "command-control." This is no longer ideal leadership behavior in many organizations given the increasingly diverse and rapidly changing workplace. People have greater expectations for their own development and life quality, and the autocratic leader is at an increasing disadvantage.

THE AUTHENTIC ADVANTAGE FOR
REACHING TRUE POTENTIAL

This image of needing to be over-bearing can also cause some men to hold back their more empathetic authentic personality. Due to cultural stereotyping, there is often a social taboo against men displaying empathetic feelings, particularly within the business and leadership context. In a January 2010 research article by Birgit Derntl et al. entitled "Multidimensional Assessment of Empathetic Abilities, ", data analyses revealed no significant gender differences in behavioral performance as it relates to empathetic abilities; however, females rated themselves as more empathic than males in the self-report questionnaires. A functional MRI study was performed with 12 females and 12 males, while measuring tasks to assess emotion recognition, perspective taking and affective responsiveness as well as self-report empathy questionnaires. In this type of study, fMRI testing reveals physiologic reactions within the brain; this is more objective than subjective self-reporting assessments alone. As an executive coach and physician, I can attest to the fact that on many occasions I have seen the empathetic side of men emerge when they are not "performing" in public. It is often a type of stigma for men to be "empathetic" and good listeners. I also have to say that women do not have a corner on empathy or listening skill and that universally, not all women are empathetic. Once again, stereotyping limits the depth of our true individual human potential in general. Generalizing behavior based on gender is a form of prejudging and bias. The good news is, thanks to neuroplasticity research, we have objective data to demonstrate that with intentional mindfulness practices, both genders can cultivate higher levels of empathy.

What must be taken into consideration regarding this "left-brained" keep-emotion-out-of-it behavior is that this behavior is not confined to men. Research has shown that over-activity of the left brain's conscious "focused attention" and "keep it logical" tendency can create a type of interference with the more intuitive, empathetic right-brain. The right-brain capacities for empathy and insight cannot as readily engage under these types of cognitive conditions. I do want to emphasize here that the left and right brain hemispheres are designed to complement, not duplicate each side's functionality. Also, discovery of the relationships between those areas of the brain that are associated with a given emotional response is an ongoing process, and these relationships are not rigidly and unchangeably defined. Men and women readily have access to both hemispheres; however, nurture will impact nature.

As an example of how so-called male, "'left-brained" thinkers can evolve, I once met a self-described "rigid thinking" engineer who claimed that he previously had challenges with intuition and emotional connection but was able to exercise his brain in a way that put him out of his comfort zone. Ultimately, he became quite intuitive and highly empathic. This example is supported by research that substantiates neuroplasticity. In other words, we cannot say that men are "hardwired" to be aggressive or lacking empathy. I will present more references regarding this research in chapter three: Leading with the Brain in Mind. Likewise, there are plenty of strategic, linear-thinking women; I know many. Men are not the only human beings who can behave in a "traditionally male" manner; I too once generally behaved in this way. Given the power of "nurture over nature," even if one is currently wired this way, there is hard evidence that one can literally change one's brain. For example, findings from a study from Harvard University Department of Neurology, led by Pascual-Leone et al. and entitled "The Plastic Human Brain Cortex," support the theory that behavior can lead to changes in our brain circuitry and changes in brain circuitry can lead to behavioral modifications. This study revealed that actually practicing fingering movements on the piano *and* imagining these same movements could literally change the neuro-architecture of the brain. This is a dynamic process. Our thinking can change our behavior and our brain and these changes are not irreversible. Mental agility can be developed.

THE BLAME GAME LIMITS LEADERSHIP POTENTIAL

Even assigning blame to testosterone for aggressive behavior has come into question. There is new research suggesting that an increase in testosterone is a *result* of aggressive behavior, and *not the cause* of it. This is known as "The Challenge Hypothesis," which I will address later in the book. I know from my own behavioral evolution that aggression can be a learned response that is often developed as a reaction to some perceived threat in the environment. It can be unconsciously adopted as a behavior pattern in the personality, which is what happened to me as a teenager. Fortunately, thanks to the ability to change our minds and behaviors, I no longer deal with this tendency. It's really not about gender; it's about human beings needing to evolve and grow. In short, *we can retrain our brains.*

While blog titles such as "Are Women Better Leaders than Men?" catch a lot of attention and are interesting, it is time to go deeper and address the root of this issue. We need to leave behind outdated conventional thinking and begin, as Henry David Thoreau so eloquently expressed in the quote in the Introduction, *"striking at the root."* According to a *Harvard Business Review* blog posted by Jack Zenger and Joseph Folkman on March 15, 2012, their research found that women are rated higher in fully 12 of the 16 competencies that affect outstanding leadership. I agree with their final conclusion that leadership skills are strongly correlated to organizational success factors such as retaining talent, satisfying customers, engaging employees and profitability.

I would also add that, regardless of gender, men and women are able to tap into the neuroplasticity of their brains to develop their leadership gaps, and they do it in a way that is unique to their own personality styles. Neither gender enjoys a monopoly when it comes to the list of "The Top 16 Competencies Top Leaders Most Exemplify," which was used as a part of this study. That being said, why are we even comparing gender? This is not a gender issue; it is a human race issue.

Based on the way our brain forms memory and creates habit patterns, **one explanation of why this gender argument is so appealing could simply be that the "Battle of the Sexes" is an old social paradigm.** Sometimes it is easier to point a finger and place blame than it is to deal with our own personal growth. While there are some differences between hormone levels and other areas of biological functioning, what I am specifically addressing in this book is research regarding the brain, biology, and cognitive development as these relate to leadership behavior. In this regard, there is plenty of evidence that the "gender effects" on leadership arguments are not scientifically substantiated. All women do not behave the same; neither do all men. Being able to address ourselves as individuals instead of as a "gender" would help us to redirect out attention to move forward, which is important considering the global challenges we are facing.

OUR "STORYTELLING" BRAIN CAN CHANGE

If these gender stereotypes are counterproductive to our efforts to lead more effectively, why do they still persist? This longstanding gender argument, despite neuroplasticity research, is a symptom of our "storytelling brain," which is unwittingly wired in a way that can keep us "stuck." If we want to be more effective as leaders in our ever-changing environment and make the impact we desire to make, it will be necessary to start telling ourselves better stories by understanding *how* to retrain our own brain and mind. In other words, we must learn *how* to better self-manage. The "brain storylines" that we create, as science has shown, will lead to our "reality." These stories become wired into our brain and will create our habitual way of showing up in the world. Until we address this new opportunity and learn to change our thinking (our mindset), we will keep creating our current reality.

Reality is merely an illusion; albeit a very persistent one.

— Albert Einstein

Our reality is persistent because before now we did not understand much about our own brain and our ability to purposely adapt to change. We *can* turn our attention toward creating a "new reality." We can learn how to optimize our whole brain with more self-awareness. We *can* learn how to become a more engaging leader with less effort when we learn how to effectively tap into the "inner technology" of our own brains. It is in the *"What we don't know that we don't know"* that we will find the solution to the gender and leadership argument. After all, this is what innovation and creativity are all about. **The obstacles to overcome are the outdated beliefs regarding leadership models and gender stereotyping.** Stereotyping, when accepted by an individual, can hinder his or her own personal and professional development. This is true for both men and women. The brain is adept at creating "self-fulfilling prophecies." The better we understand this principle, the easier it will be for team members to deal with dysfunction and more quickly create healthier, sustainable business models.

THE WHOLE IS GREATER THAN UNINTEGRATED PARTS

In our pursuit of more highly evolved leadership styles, we must become aware of the need to integrate our whole life—work/life integration—because each of us is a single, whole unit person. After all, you take you with you wherever you go. The separation between work and personal life is an artificial one. What would our lives look like if we were confident and fulfilled in our work as well as our lives outside the office? How would it change our sense of purpose and meaning if those we worked with were less defensive and insensitive, and our organization fostered trust, personal development, and a culture of harmony? How would this impact customer service and profits? Do you think that this type of scenario would encourage employees to be inspired to come to work every Monday morning? We can learn how to realize more of our brain potential in a way that constructively serves our growth and development as a leader and as a human being.

And yet, this question of leadership and gender is only part of the story. It is a symbol that our definition of leadership is evolving—*and needs to evolve*—in order to be in sync with our changing world. By recognizing the need for constant personal growth as leaders, we will be better equipped to embrace change and innovation in real-time. When confronted with team dysfunction or new global competition, the fact is that the more capable we are of dealing with conflict or collaborating with other departments within the organizational structure, the more profitable our businesses will be.

If we are to successfully adapt to this ever-increasing pace of change and evolving work environment, we will need to address the individual at work in terms of personal growth and development. This applies to both the leader and the team members; however, it must begin with the leader. Both men and women are being required to be less reactive and more engaging and proactive. *There is a need for leaders who are willing to learn how to slow down and reflect before charging into action without clarification of direction and values.* In general, most people in Western culture over-value activity and "doing" to a fault. It has become a brain-wired habit pattern and this is at the root of stress and lack of creativity. Without brain awareness, it is a slow and arduous process to lead this kind of change. We will need to come to terms with the brain research that supports the need for reflection and restoration for optimal performance. This balancing effect from the "right-brain" re-energizes and helps one to become more effective.

DIFFERENT RESULTS REQUIRE DIFFERENT BEHAVIORS

Innovation requires reflection and engagement of the mind and heart of individuals. These behavior changes are difficult to make if one believes he or she is "hardwired" and has no information about how to "retrain their brain" or change the story they have been telling themselves. Similar to me, many controlling leaders actually have the capacity and desire to be engaging and empathic. Without understanding how to retrain the brain, current leadership assessment tools will continue to label behavior based on superficial behavioral parameters of personality. While traditional personality tests are useful to this conversation and often do bring some self-awareness regarding the differences team members exhibit in the world, they do not inform an individual about "how" to *change* or adjust their personality, or even inform a person that they can. If this is not specifically addressed, these tests can reinforce the belief that, "that's just the way I am." I have observed my various personality assessment results evolve over time as I changed my self-image from the inside out. This is not about faking anything; it is about evolving one's consciousness to a higher level. It is about reconnecting one's mind and heart and living from a space of authenticity.

Research demonstrates that members of organizations want to contribute, have more autonomy, and desire to expand the vision of their life beyond the robotic, "business as usual" behavior that has previously dominated the corporate world. They are looking for values-based, purpose-driven leadership. However, this will require innovation at both the personal and the corporate organizational level.

GETTING TO KNOW OUR BRAIN

Changing perception intentionally begins within. Current research reveals that fully 95% of what runs our daily life is outside of our conscious awareness. For most people, only 5% is under conscious control. This is one reason why willpower is not as effective. Willpower is a function of conscious choice and our conscious mind is very distracted by information overload and life on the verge of overwhelm. By better understanding that the part of the mind that runs 95% of our life is the subconscious mind, we can better reprogram our outdated habitual thinking that determines the actions we ultimately take at the office and at home.

Leaders will need to change their brain wiring in order to be able to adapt to change and to innovate without generating so much resistance and discomfort. I would argue, based on my own experience and how I have seen my clients change their perception as it relates to stress and fear over short periods of time, that the brain is not hard-wired naturally for the level of excessive fear and stress that people are experiencing in the world today. In fact, there is research underway to support this very notion. I will refer to this in chapter four: The Divided Brain and the Battle of the Sexes. It is time to stop assigning blame to the "reptilian brain" in our effort to account for our exceedingly high levels of stress. When we understand *how* we feed or starve this part of our brain, we can better manage it. Fear dumbs us down and creates resistance. Using our storytelling brain, we have wired a story—a perception that causes us to see life as more stress-filled and competitive than it needs to be. Our current "management" paradigm of the "commanding" boss feeds into the fear that triggers this less than ideal, unproductive behavioral response.

When we are sufficiently self-aware to take the necessary action, this new paradigm shift allows us to call upon, in our own authentic personality-based way, whatever is needed or required in the moment. While it is easy to say men are like this or women are like that, here is the reality: we are being asked from a global perspective to adapt rapidly. We either respond effectively, or we will become irrelevant and lose to competitive forces that are better able to adapt. To illustrate this point, consider the story of Kodak film, a brand and history that should have easily led and captured the digital camera market but failed to do so. Also, recall the Blockbuster Video example referred to previously—a company that refused to innovate and evolve its model and, as a result, lost its competitive advantage and is now bankrupt. We can either evolve or get run over in the process. Evolutionary change waits for no one and will eventually override human resistance. Why wait for history to repeat itself to the detriment of our society?

Need more empathy and new creative, imaginative ideas? If so, you can call upon your right brain hemisphere. Need more linear structure and analytical process? If so, you can call upon your left-brain hemisphere. Leadership is not a gender-based proposition. Stepping into your leadership potential requires courage from the heart and spirit, and it requires you to take a look at your beliefs and behaviors to uncover the "blind spots" that are holding you back from making a greater impact.

What can we do to transcend these stereotypical models in order to lead with greater purpose and to inspire those around us to fulfill their potential? In order to adapt to and rise to the challenge of our changing times, we will need to address, not so much an outer roadblock, but an inner one—a roadblock within our own selves. We will need to change our minds in order to create a "mindset for success." The environment has changed and old ways of thinking cannot solve the current problems that we face. What we know from science is that there is much truth to the old saying "as a man [or woman] thinketh in his [her] heart, so is he [she]." How we think and feel determines *how* we see. Perception truly can become reality.

Leadership is about personal growth and development within the context of the work environment and our everyday life. Leaders lead change. Integrating new learning within the context of work has been a part of the challenge with leadership development training. Simply scheduling a few off-site training sessions without application into real life is likely to garner limited or no results. Also, only learning tactical skill sets without an evolving mindset is not sustainable. One lesson we should have begun to learn by now in our turbulent times is that change is constant and does not wait for permission to occur. The more self-aware we become of our blind spots and how we are causing them, the sooner we will be able to become more resilient, adaptable, and confident leaders. Let us turn now to uncovering the root of the inauthentic behaviors that are holding us back, so we can begin to grow our leadership skills from the inside out.

Key Points

- We have overused our Survival Brain and we are not well acquainted with our Thrival Brain—neuroscience is the potent path to engaging our Thrival Brain faster and easier.

- Cognitive development is not biologically "hardwired"—environment greatly influences our brain's wiring patterns for behavior.

- Neuroplasticity is our ability to consciously "retrain our brain"—we can literally "neuro-reinvent" ourselves.

- Men and women can learn emotional intelligence and fill in their leadership gaps around vision, engagement, strategy, problem-solving, and innovation as well as maintain clear boundaries for accountability and authority—self-awareness is key.

- Whole brain integration leads to a healthier work/life integration, reduction of stress, and an increase in fulfillment, productivity, and purpose.

Reflect: Inquiring Mind

1. How does predominantly focusing on the past limit your vision for the future?

2. How do you account for situations and people that do not align with "how life is" by your definition? Do you explain the situation away or do you ask yourself "why" you are not open to seeing each person or situation with fresh eyes—beyond blind spots?

3. What does behavior change mean to you? If you dread or resist it, why? If you embrace it and see it as a positive, why?

4. In light of the fact that the brain is able to adapt to change and rewire itself with your intention, do you think it will be possible to change behavior easier with this new knowledge, "on demand"? If not, why?

5. How does behavior impact the efficiency and effectiveness of your organization?

Envision Possibilities

1. What would the workplace look like if people were seen and developed as persons capable of being challenged in productive ways versus leaving them in jobs that keep them disengaged?

2. How would the workplace climate feel with male leaders who are good listeners and are able to situationally "read" people accurately and with compassion? Would this raise loyalty?

3. How would your profits be impacted if employees were enthusiastic about coming to work? Imagine the efficiency of an organization built on trust and cooperation instead of competition and "battles." Thinking differently depends on getting your mind out of the box with divergent considerations. Can you *see* this in your mind's eye (imagination)?

CHAPTER TWO

GENDER INAUTHENTICITY LIMITS LEADERSHIP POTENTIAL

The best time to plant a tree is twenty years ago.
The second best time is today.

— Chinese Proverb

DEVELOPING HEALTHY, AUTHENTIC ROOTS— IT IS NOT TOO LATE

T he root of much of our inauthentic behavior and personality as leaders is molded by our culture. These assumptions are then wired into our minds by our "storytelling" brain. We create stories regarding not only gender, but also age and cultural bias that can make us ineffective in engaging a growingly diverse workforce. It is our individual interpretation about what we are told that becomes the basis for how we come to see others and ourselves. The brain and nervous system are nature's way of giving us the ability to navigate socially and make choices. This is the basis of perception and how we form our beliefs. Individuals form the culture, and the culture then becomes the invisible force that takes over and reinforces the status quo. The question now becomes, "What can women and men do to take back the 'Steering Wheels of their

35

minds' to move forward in a direction that produces sustainable and dynamic leadership, performance, and well-being?" One answer is to learn how to "NeuroReInvent" ourselves. While I don't want to oversimplify this complex issue, one powerful way to accomplish this, which holds great impact, is to begin understanding the capacity of our amazing brains to change themselves and thus change the way we see ourselves and the world around us. Research shows that it is ***the meaning we assign*** *to our thoughts, feelings, and experiences that matters to the quality of our decisions, the actions we take, and our lives.* It is important for me to define what I mean by "inauthentic," and I do so by beginning with the context for what is "authentic."

The Meaning of Authenticity and Inauthenticity

By authentic, I am referring to what has meaning for an individual in terms of the person's values, natural gifts and inclinations, life purpose, and (possibly) life mission. It is what is genuinely and wholeheartedly important to "you." If perceived personal threat and social conditioning were excluded, authentic behavior would be what feels natural, is uninhibited, and is "energy efficient," e.g., it is easier to do because it "just feels right." As long as the behavior does not inflict physical harm and is within the limits of the law as it relates to civil rights, it would be desirable to express.

What typically happens is that the vast majority of human beings, from a very young age, begin trying to fit into the best mold that serves their security, love, and self-esteem needs. (This is even reflected in Abraham Maslow's Hierarchy of Needs—though as an idea, the concept is ancient). Human beings will tend to repress their natural joy for the sake of belonging and, of course, since young children cannot care for themselves, the physical world of "nurture" often trumps the inner world of "nature." What we know now from brain science is that how we wire our brains will be recorded in our bodies at a "cellular" memory level, going into the "subconscious"—out of our conscious awareness—until triggered. This begins the journey of forming behaviors that may be incongruent or inauthentic with *"who we really are"* in our heart and spirit in order to conform instead to gender roles and feelings of acceptance by the prescribed social group.

Recently released books such as Facebook's COO Sheryl Sandberg's *Lean In* and historian Stephanie Coontz's *A Strange Stirring (*a book which revisits the classic *The Feminine Mystique)*, point to and document the rigidity in gender role assignments and how our society perpetuates the myths related to these assignments. These books also reference the internal voices with which women often struggle—voices that contribute to self-sabotage. Sheryl Sandberg mentions in her book that she was teased as a child because of her "bossiness." To this day, she relates struggles with feelings of shame when her family still teases her about it. To her point regarding double standards, this probably would not be so "funny" if she were a boy. This also serves to illustrate how we store "cellular memory." Specifically, in her book, Ms. Sandberg confides that she still "slightly feels ashamed of my behavior" when people laugh at her family accounts of her childhood leadership behaviors. The fact that Sheryl continues to operate within her authenticity instead of pulling back to conform is a testament to her courage and determination to, as I would say, "Be YOU, *Magnificently."*

I also have experienced what Sheryl Sandberg refers to because it relates to feelings I have had in the past when a family story from my childhood was used to tease me. I felt ashamed even though the original incident occurred decades earlier. The absence of this shame now is one reason why I know that we really can "retrain" our brains and change our physiologic reaction to these old perceptions and memories. I know this because I have done it. I can assure you, there are no more cellular memory triggers for me, at least as this relates to family stories.

Historical Development of Inauthentic Role Playing

How does gender-based inauthentic role-playing behavior get started within the context of our personal development and social life? Social Role Theory, offered by Northwestern University researcher Alice H. Eagly, suggests that almost all behavioral differences between males and females stem from cultural stereotypes about gender (how males and females are "supposed" to act) and the resulting social roles that are taught to children.

Until the 1960s, the roles of men and women were quite strictly and, even when necessary, artificially prescribed. These prescriptions for male and female roles inhibited the true potential of both men and women. Men and women were then, and often still are (even if unwittingly), conditioned to accept social personality behavior that may not align with their highest vision for self-image, or is not in the best interest of those around them. There were and still are complex forces behind these generationally presumed teachings; but suffice it to say that "perception is reality" to the mind and brain once something is accepted as true. These historical social dynamics are the source of gender behavioral stereotypes, and are the roots that form the gender and leadership arguments.

I often hear in leadership gender arguments that men and women are different because our ancestors demonstrated certain role tendencies. It goes like this: "Men were hunters and women were gatherers, so this is why men make better leaders, are more assertive, and are natural providers." There are several flaws in this argument, but I will simply list only three:

1. Historically, one can find cultures in which women also were hunters.

2. Due to social role-playing, women met with severe resistance when attempting to enter "a man's world," which was socially defined.

3. Women generally were not allowed to self-actualize; woman's role was to take care of others and neglect her own needs.

Given the fact that research demonstrates that the brain will wire to help a person adapt to the "reality" that leads to survival, it is quite understandable that women complied and became the gatherers—whether it was authentic or not. Our mammalian brain, or "social-brain," is very vigilant in attending to our survival need to "belong" based on how *we* perceive the social threat. Likewise, a man would have likely been ridiculed and rejected if he did not "act like a man," "hunting and providing" as deemed politically correct. It is not likely that he was given the option to be a gatherer unless he was physically incapable of hunting. This type of "role assigning" still goes on today. The point is, the assumption that men are hunters and women are gatherers is not based in biology; it is based in culture.

Balance is important; ***this is not about men or women dominating.*** The ideal structure for a peaceful and productive world is to allow the best to be expressed in both men and women, rather than to be repressed out of fear of rejection and social stereotyping. There is strength in a diversity of leadership styles. Having exhibited "Command-Control" behavior myself—a stereotypically male behavior style—I know that one's personality can be a learned response since earlier in life I was quite passive. Fortunately, I have also unlearned it—sustainably. I now choose to be both assertive and receptive in alignment with my own leadership style when it is deemed appropriate by my own judgment in the moment. Also, because our brains are so adaptable, I know that we are able to access a variety of behavioral styles that contradict social gender expectations. In order to effect change, we need to know our historical roots. Let us explore deeper this idea of "Leadership and Gender" as it relates to history and current brain research.

A "WOMAN'S PLACE"

These cultural beliefs and attitudes about each of the sexes still pervade organizational culture and have led to the stereotypes and attitudes we see in our conference rooms and workplaces today. While these stereotypes tend to limit both men and women in different ways, one limitation that is most pervasive and impactful is related to women as caregivers. Many women are expected to be empathetic, which now has been shown to be beneficial in the workplace in many situations. Yet, this type of artificial role assignment can also be detrimental in situations that require assertiveness or the ability to construct healthy boundaries. Women are much less likely than men to take credit for what is rightfully theirs, and they are often expected to act in more passive, prescribed ways than are men. This can hinder a woman's confidence as a leader. If a woman acts in the traditional leadership style of "command-control," she is commonly ostracized; yet when men behave this way, it is too often overlooked or ignored. Clearly, this is a double standard. Quite frankly, in today's workplace, one's access to the leadership style repertoire needs to broaden. "Traditional" autocratic leadership tends to discourage people from making their best contributions.

Personality Conditioning: Nurture vs. Nature

Historically, women were expected to be "behind the throne" and to devote themselves to helping and serving others, even at their own expense. Over time, many experts have engaged in ongoing research that addressed perceived "differences" between men and women's behaviors and, more often than not, the empirical conclusions drawn are assumed to be attributable to biological differences. Little did we know at the time how pliable the brain is, and how cooperative it can be, given an intent to change and adapt to the environment. It is quite remarkable to learn from science the influential role that "nurture" plays in determining how "nature" manifests in the life of an individual human being, including behavioral and personality development. The role of women that is still typically presumed and often applies, is that they should be supportive, empathetic, cooperative, gentle and, in some cultures, passive and submissive. Women were and still are unconsciously expected to anticipate the feelings and needs of others and put these ahead of their own needs.

It's not that there is anything wrong or "bad" with serving others. I believe that we all have a place when it comes to being of service to others; the issue is what is truly purposeful for the individual. What is the real inherent talent and place for the individual regardless of gender? Women historically have been accorded an expectation that they serve in the roles of wife, mother, nurse, volunteer, community server, teacher, and assistant. Again, these are all honorable roles and are not to be devalued; the key word, however, is "expectation." Every female is not wired from her authentic heart to take on these roles. A female, just as a male, may have other plans to serve in different ways.

Some girls, before conditioned, speak of aspiring to roles that have in past generations traditionally been dominated by males, such as doctor, CEO, or attorney—even president of the United States. Historically, few girls have had the courage to follow through and jump the many hurdles placed before them. Perhaps a woman may also want to be a mother *and* a CEO. Yet society has made it very challenging, and then has tended to heap guilt upon the woman who dared to step outside of the gender definition box. To make matters worse, all too often, science and biology were used to explain and justify social rules for engagement.

Relationship and Rejection

As a matter of history, women could not vote less than a century ago in the United States. Under these conditions, it was nearly impossible for women to start and run their own companies. What did biology have to do with this? If women are able to start and run companies now, they could have done so in the past. But they were physically and legally prohibited from doing so in many cases, and certainly, at the very least, faced rejection and ostracism. Of course, considering that social rejection was often dangerous to one's survival in the past, it is not surprising that most women conformed to the social norm. Fear of rejection, however, is not limited to women. On the one hand, women have tended to fear rejection based on relationship because relationship was equated to "survival." On the other hand, men's fear of rejection tended to be hidden behind the mask of "power" or the need to feel "in control." The point here is that these stereotypical behavioral forces are not rooted in biology; *they are rooted in culture.*

Relationship and Leadership

Judy B. Rosener's (1990) *Harvard Business Review* article entitled, **"Ways Women Lead,"** also makes reference to this point. Rosener makes the point that women's socialization encourages interaction with others. I think it is safe to say that women are expected to be the nurturers in society whether it feels authentic for the individual woman or not. This kind of leadership comes easily to women because society aggressively encourages females to be caretakers, attuned to the feelings and needs of those around them.

The need for bonding and relationship is a function of mammals, not just the female human being. Culture made the difference in how the dance was done. Men need relationship as well. It is this need to recognize the power of relationship and connection that is now emerging within the context of organizational efficiency and, in many ways, this is at the root of our leadership crisis. The need to astutely relate to others has now become an obstacle for many men to culturally overcome if they want to be more engaging, inspirational leaders. Of course, there are women who will also need to develop more of their relational skills as well. And, clearly, there are men who are already well equipped to bond in a healthy manner and engage with others. In order to set the historical context, I have purposely focused along "gender lines." *In truth, neither empathy nor aggressive behavior is strictly limited to one gender or the other.*

My intention is not to state that there are no biological differences between men and women; *my intention is to dispel the myth that biology determines cognitive development as it relates to leadership ability.* There is an important distinction between biology and cultural conformity, especially in light of what we now know about the ability of our brain to adapt in ways that create "self-fulfilling prophecy."

ADAPTING TO "SURVIVAL OF THE FITTEST"

Men, who have dominated the corporate landscape, had to play to the theme of "survival of the fittest" in the workplace and the world, which really is only a paradigm. This is a carryover from historical conditioning dictating that a man must be the "hero," or that a "real man" acts aggressively, much like the stereotype of the rugged cowboy. This paradigm promotes male leaders who are poor listeners and hence do not grow as leaders. This style of leadership has also been a significant source of employee disengagement. It is a hindrance to innovation and implementation as well. Certainly, *competition is a part of life, but so is cooperation.* In fact, the cooperative nature of the ecological balance of the earth supports growth and life, something we seem to have forgotten. Yet, men had to appear tough, insensitive, and "in control" or they too would be under threat of ridicule and ostracism. These are the other roots of the "command-control" leader. Women have been allowed to access the gentler, cooperative sides of the human psyche. But these traits are now considered important in our rapidly evolving world and are needed for healthy emotional intelligence (EQ or EI).

Research demonstrates that leaders and professionals with high emotional intelligence typically out-perform those with only a high IQ. Once the fundamental skills are acquired, EQ wins out over IQ when performance results are compared. EQ is an advantage to have in all areas of professional performance, including sales, marketing, strategy, and innovation. *This integration of strength and gentleness, individualism and community, and EQ/IQ balance are traits that are accessible to all human beings regardless of gender. What's more, they are needed for resilient, visionary, and effective 21ˢᵗ century leadership—regardless of gender.*

As an example, I was invited to attend a group luncheon with some corporate women. At my table, three women held prestigious MBA degrees from a very well-known institution. One particular woman, who had been laid off after a very long sales career at IBM, shared with me how at meetings, men would physically spread out and take up space with their arms and legs. They also tended to aggressively dominate the conversation. She explained how she repressed some of her own self-expression for fear of being seen as "domineering." Yet afterwards, on more than one occasion, she said the male from the meeting would assume a totally different persona when not "on guard." She found that there were many instances where men showed evidence that they were capable of compassion and empathy, but they wore masks of "bravado" during meetings. I've found this to be true in some situations myself.

Belief in a "zero sum gain" model of competition supports "traditional" corporate leadership styles due to the corresponding belief that winners are those who are dominant, aggressive, and able to exert power over others. In fact, some leaders behave in a "macho" way in order to fulfill the perception leaders "should behave" in this fashion. Well—male leaders, that is.

Yet in today's society, in order to engage the most skilled and the brightest, leaders will need to engage the heart and mind in order to cultivate cooperation and intellectual growth. Individuals want their self-worth enhanced and honored, not whittled away by a self-centered, authoritarian leader. A growing number of people want to be seen, heard, and developed; not simply told what to do. If this paradigm of "survival of the fittest" does not evolve, it could be the very thing that threatens our survival itself, which is ironic indeed.

This journey to change and growth begins by having the courage to address the root of the problem as it relates to beliefs and behavior that impact the modern day leader, whether the person is female or male. Role-playing inhibits our natural gifts and talents as a leader. It can keep us from being emotionally intelligent and connecting with team members. It can create blind spots that block innovation and effectiveness. Men have been conditioned to play the survival of the fittest game and women have been conditioned to be the caregivers. Both of these stereotypes are established by the culture and limit leadership skill. Do not underestimate the power of the brain to create self-fulfilling prophecy and form blind spots to keep you stuck in the "reality" that you have created for yourself. Your experience, of course, is "real" to you and needs to be honored, not shamed. You cannot evolve what you refuse to examine. Yet, the question again is, can we retrain our brains to become more effective leaders, regardless of gender?

> *The curious paradox is that when I accept*
> *myself just as I am, then I can change.*
>
> — Carl Rogers

IS IT NATURE'S WAY?: CHALLENGING THE MYTHS

Yes, we can retrain our brains to become more effective leaders. In order to do so, we need to become clear about how our environments can mold our minds. Thanks to brain research, it is becoming much more difficult to blame our behavior on "Mother Nature." This again is good news because we can take responsibility—*"response-ability"*—to a whole new level. It will help you as a leader, on both a personal and professional level, to be able to uncover your purpose, true core values, and talents. When you know who you are and work from your core power, you can be your personal best instead of trying to align with standards that feel faked and forced upon you. You can live a more purposeful and fulfilling life at home and at the office. Before I proceed, I will address some of the myths that are circulating—often disguised as scientific research regarding biology and behavior. Following this analysis, you can more easily observe how biology does not predestinate your leadership capacity.

Implicit Behavior and Gender Role-playing

I have read a number of arguments suggesting that parents do not believe in gender differences; yet, their children seemed to "naturally" play with stereotypical toys and align with prescribed gender roles. What they do not recognize or cite is the power of "implicit" behavior. A four-year-old girl named Riley gives us a beautiful example of this. In a YouTube video that went viral and has experienced over 4 million views, she, in her eloquent, four-year-old manner, questions why in toy stores, girls are segregated to the "pink stuff" and boys to the superhero section. As she accurately states, some girls like superheroes and some boys like the pink stuff. Wisdom out of the mouth of babes! Parents are not aware of how their own behavior is confusing the child; they are also unaware of the fact that children do not live in a bubble. The gender roles of grandparents, other relatives, and friends impact children as well as the general culture and media. These observations then get passed off as "genetic or brain wiring."

Children pick up unconscious body language from parents regarding race and gender bias. It is not what you say; it is what you do. Ralph Waldo Emerson is believed to have said: *"What you do speaks so loudly that I cannot hear what you say."* We all know the "do as I say, not as I do" adage. Children generally follow by example; hence the power of implicit behavior. Even the parent himself or herself is not aware of their unconscious gender-conditioned behavior. The implicit overrides what we think we believe on the surface at a conscious level. That being said, even the best-intentioned parents influence their children's behavior unconsciously. Research has been conducted that substantiated this factor as well (Friedman, Leaper, & Bigler, 2007).

Is It All in the Eyes?

Another prevailing myth is that newborn baby girls are more prone to relationship and connection because they "gaze into the eyes" of others longer than boy babies. This also has been used as an argument for why women are naturally more empathetic than men. What has been shown is that researcher bias plays a role when the tester knows he/she is examining a boy versus girl baby in a newborn nursery. When the babies where dressed in a gender-neutral outfit instead of the traditional "pink or blue," and when other factors such as stimulus and response objects were standardized, there were no gender differences found between males and females and attention to facial tracking. Boys responded just as well as girls. I therefore agree with the following statement made by Rebecca Jordan-Young (2010) in her book *Brainstorm:*

> *The evidence for hormonal sex differentiation of the human brain better resembles a hodge-podge pile than a solid structure.... Once we have cleared the rubble, we can begin to build newer, more scientific stories about human development.*

Empathy and Relationship: For Women Only?

Empathy can be cultivated, and one cannot assign it to gender alone as if it is automatically fully developed at birth. For men and women, empathy is influenced by culture. Empathy is not necessarily a feature of all relationships either. Just having a proclivity toward relationship does not mean that the relationships are healthy and functional. I want to emphasize this fact because, even though some teen-aged girls are prone to focusing on relationship, this doesn't always equate with empathy. Consider, for example, how unkindly some teen girls can treat each other. This is a harmful and troublesome problem during the adolescent and high school years. I was once a teenage girl and I raised a daughter, so I know this unkind behavioral tendency is a real phenomenon. Just being relationship prone doesn't mean one is emotionally intelligent.

I've already mentioned how the socialization process steers women toward relationship and men toward commerce as the foundation for one's sense of self-identity. This is not to say that a given man or a woman could not have an authentic tendency toward relationship; however, this is to say that gender is not the basis for this tendency. Neither all women nor all men gravitate toward relationship with others as a dominant social style. It's important that people choose according to their preference instead of a prescribed gender label; otherwise, prejudice (pre-judgment) will be the *modus operandi*.

> *It's never too late to be what you might have been.*
>
> — George Eliot

While there is controversy over the origin of this quote, it is most often ascribed to Eliot. Since it does speak to "neuroplasticity," I see it as appropriate for this conversation on more than one level. George Eliot was the nom de plume for Mary Ann Evans, an English novelist who lived during the Victorian period. She said she used a male pen name so that she would not be stereotypically pushed into writing romance novels, as women of her time were typically charged to do. You see, women have their own individual ways of expression, as do men, even historically. It's just not often that we can find examples such as this that demonstrate the power of culture to influence behavior. Mary Ann had to have confidence and courage to buck the culture, a trait that was not encouraged in women, then or now, in many circles.

[For more information concerning this area, you can refer to a 2007 article by Alison Nash and Giordana Grossi titled "Picking Barbie™'s Brain: Inherent Sex Differences in Scientific Ability?" and to books on sex differences offered in the resource section.]

CHILDHOOD EDUCATION AND LEADERSHIP DEVELOPMENT

Dr. Lise Eliot is a biologist and neuroscientist who indicated that when she began her research for her 2009 book, *Pink Brain, Blue Brain*, she expected it would be simple to find studies that validated the assumptions made about boys' "blue" brains and girls' "pink" brains to help explain differences in academic performance. She found otherwise:

But what I found, after an exhaustive search was surprisingly little solid evidence of sex differences in children's brains.... The reality, judging by current research, is that the brains of boys and girls are more similar than their well-described behavioral differences would indicate.... Simply put, your brain is what you do with it. (pp. 5–6)

Dr. Eliot's finding aligns with other articles published by cognitive neuroscientists that I have read over time and in the preparation of this book. Due to the recent findings about the "neuroplasticity" of the brain, we know that the brain changes itself based on experience and even thought (thinking) alone. There is no evidence for "inherent hardwiring" to account for cognitive performance; the environment has a tremendous impact on the direction that a child will take in developing their true potential. In boys and girls, nurture can support or impede nature. This has implications for our educational systems as well. Girls are often implicitly discouraged from believing in and pursuing their math or science strength, or other areas that have been traditional pursuits for boys. Boys supposedly have less verbal skill. These assumptions are made by the educational system. Females now account for 60% of college graduates. It is not in the best interest of society for boys or girls to dominate the educational system. Perhaps the system itself needs reforming.

Optimal creativity has been found to be associated with teams that are balanced and diversified in gender and abilities. This issue of optimal team function, where there is a gender balance, is discussed in the research of Avivah Wittenberg-Cox, author of the book, ***How Women Mean Business***. Our educational system needs to evolve if it is to support the potential of girls and boys as human beings, not genders. They are the emerging leaders of tomorrow. Also, it is interesting that, in the business world, just the opposite imbalance in gender is noted to an even greater extreme when it comes to high level leadership positions. While females fare better overall within the educational system, within the corporate world, men far outnumber women in terms of executive level leadership positions. Men comprise 80–90% of executive level leadership in corporate organizations. This is true despite the fact that women account for at least 50–60% of entry-level professionals. These perceptual biases regarding leadership ability and their roots are the focus of this book. Corporations, like the educational systems, need to evolve their models, not just for the benefit of the individual, but for the welfare of society at large if we are to continue successfully innovating and adapting to change. True potential human capital needs to be developed, not thwarted by historical social bias. We need the intellectual and emotional capital of both men and women to be available from the most qualified individual. The leadership advantage will belong to those who can adapt and expand their potential instead of falling prey to "self-fulfilling" prophecies.

WHICH IS FIRST...CHICKEN OR EGG?

Finally, I want to touch on the area of hormones. Often I hear that our hormones are responsible for our emotional reactivity or for our tendency to be aggressive. This is yet another contentious area of debate in the gender differences conversation. Since our perception about our environment molds our brain, and it is our reaction to a situation that triggers our physiology, it is getting much tougher to blame our reactions on our hormones. For example, testosterone historically is blamed for male aggression and estrogen is blamed for female "emotionalism"—often a subjective attribute. Sure, the increased presence of one of these hormones may play a role in our behavior, but research is now asking the question, "Does perception play a role in determining the level of circulating sex hormone?" This is a much trickier question these days than in the past, before we understood our brains as we now do.

In *Pink Brain, Blue Brain* (2009), Lise Eliot also pointed out:

Although there's some suggestion that men with constitutionally higher testosterone levels are more inclined to try to dominate others, researchers are increasingly finding that testosterone works the other way around in adults: it's more the consequence of male competition and aggression rather than the cause. (p. 268)

Once again, nurture changes nature. This new theory has been labeled the "Challenge Hypothesis." Testosterone levels apparently increase **after** an aggressive encounter is initiated or provoked. It would make sense then that if behavior revolves around an increase of testosterone, and men naturally have higher levels than women in the first place, then more testosterone would be measured with aggressive behavior. The key point to reiterate is that it is the behavior that provokes this increase. Generally speaking, changing behavior changes and reduces excessive testosterone levels in some notable instances.

I mention this simply to establish that we should not be using our hormones to stereotype or justify behavior. We can better self-manage our emotions, which affect our hormones, by becoming more brain-aware. Our perception determines whether or not the more advanced level of our brain, the neo-Cortex, is able to keep the older, less advanced levels of our brain from hijacking us. This is why self-awareness is so crucial to emotional intelligence development. Just as we don't have to understand how our cell phone works internally in order to program it, **we don't have to understand all the mechanics of our brain in order to optimize its benefits for our leadership capacities when reprogramming old beliefs and behaviors that no longer serve us. We just need to be inspired and motivated to do so.** This applies to both men and women. Let us go on now to look at how these presumed differences play out in the workplace.

GENDER AND THE WORKPLACE

Ilene H. Lang is Catalyst's president and chief executive officer. During an interview with Luisita Lopez Torregrosa of *The New York Times,* part of which was reported in Torregrosa's article entitled, "On Wall St., Gender Bias Runs Deep." In this article Ms. Lang refers to several social gender stereotypes that form assumptions within our culture. Stereotypes such as men are natural leaders and women are caretakers are common and often quoted to define gender behavior.

In the same vein, as we examine the trouble that Wall Street encountered over the past few years, we can clearly see the "macho," overly "male" leadership culture that plays out in that environment. It is demonstrative of an imbalance—mind without heart. It is not surprising then that in this Wall Street culture, females comprise only 3% of its CEOs, even though almost 50% of financial services professionals are women. **Even for men, this macho behavior is in reality a stereotype because not all intelli-**

gent, ambitious men strive solely for monetary gain without regard to the human fallout. Not all men are driven to work around the clock only to amass a great deal of money. There are, however, some men who will ignore their conscious and authentic purpose just for the sake of appearing "successful" on Wall Street for social reasons; perhaps you can also find some women doing the same.

The Inauthenticity of Stereotyping

The "Macho leadership" domineering model is one example of how inauthenticity can run our lives. This type of stereotyping certainly excludes most women, not because there are not women who could handle this type of paradigm, but studies have found that due to stereotyping, the social culture itself does not tolerate women who behave in this manner. There is an obvious double standard here. Women once again are rejected and ostracized if they behave in ways that are out of prescribed gender boxes.

Stereotyping is now interfering with societal and corporate business progress. Instead of arguing gender, we need to pay attention to the scientific research, retrain our brain, and move forward. Both genders are looking for more purpose, autonomy, and personal growth, and this will be best addressed by first teaching a person to understand him or herself better. Our "intrapersonal" relationship needs attention—that being our relationship with our self. This can be achieved by learning to "lead with the brain in mind." We can best apply our business skills and develop our emotional intelligence more sustainably and effectively by understanding how to efficiently self-manage our brain, our "inner technology" nervous system, with awareness.

Sex, Gender, and Biology

My contention is *not* that men and women are totally identical; of course our biology shows there are sex differences. Sex and gender, however, are not the same. Sex is a biological attribute defined by chromosomes and anatomy. To be objective, real science would only look at "sex" differences. Gender is a social construct, the sum of all attributes typically associated with each sex in a cultural context. Gender crosses biological lines. It is not fixed, but instead follows a spectrum of behavior traits. It changes with cultural norms. For example, people used to only think of doctors as men and women as nurses. Now, women are accepted as physicians and there is a growing number of male nurses. Admittedly, there is still evidence of social stereotyping with regard to these roles, but in my experience as one of these physicians, we've come a long way.

The danger in rooting gender myths in biology is that this implies that these differences are "hardwired" and unchangeable. Fortunately, as this relates to behavior, more and more brain science is showing that the brain is very "plastic" and can change itself through experience as well as thought and feelings alone. *The term "hardwired," when it comes to behavior, is increasingly recognized as being an erroneous concept in general usage.*

It is all too well known that some women can "act like men" and that some men can "act like women." Women do not have a corner on empathy and men do not have a corner on aggression. I am suggesting that we must rise to our next evolutionary level and stop stereotyping human beings based on their physical characteristics. The "Battle of the Sexes" is anything but benign. We are beginning to become aware of the fallout that occurs in leadership when we live from this paradigm. In this book, I am specifically referring to sex and gender. We disrespect others when we see and judge them only by external traits and then ascribe gender role behavior. It is, as Martin Luther King, Jr. said, we must "not judge others by the color of their skin [or by their gender] but by the content of their character." The arena of leadership certainly will benefit by applying this truth to sex and gender as well.

LEADERSHIP ADVANTAGE IN THE MODERN WORKPLACE

I believe that women do have an advantage in leadership style in today's workplace, not simply because we are women, but more so because "heart" behavior is more socially acceptable. Yet, do not men have a "heart" as well? Judy B. Rosener in the *Harvard Business Review* article **"Ways Women Lead"** postulates that characteristics generally considered to be "feminine" accounts for why women are succeeding in the 21st century workplace. "Macho male" leadership styles tend to lead to disengagement in today's world.

The opportunity for leadership development is to allow each individual human being social access to their whole brain as needed, and as uniquely expressed *by their unique personality.* I believe it is fear and the need to conform that is at the root of so many people's behaviors, with the pressure to conform to gender stereotypes being one of the most pervasive in our workplaces. Their behavior may not even feel like authentic expression to them. I know; I've been there, and I am still growing in self-knowledge. Learning never ends. When I was a "command-control" leader, I felt like a fake, though I would not have admitted it. I was hiding my fear behind aggression, which is a common phenomenon. In light of this, I am drawn to the words of Shawn Anchor, a Harvard researcher, taken from his book, *The Happiness Advantage*:

> *Happiness is not the belief that we don't need to change; it is the realization that we can.*

Men who reject *empathy and other "right-brain" related traits* and continue to push women into gender conformity boxes are cutting off their noses to spite their faces. *Think of the word right-brain and the word "heart" as interchangeable.* Men have access to "right-brained" styles, but they tend to under-develop them. Recall the concept of neuroplasticity. We need to reframe the connotation of the word "heart" because the right-brain is critical to innovation and creativity. Currently we stereotypically attribute the word "heart" only to females in its connotation. The brain can adapt and, quite frankly, some men's authentic personality is more prone toward these "heart-centered" traits, if the truth be told.

More often than not, the brain is performing as programmed. This prompts us as leaders to change the conversation from one that constantly compares women with men as if their biological sex is responsible. Continuing this old conversation only helps to sustain the "battle of the sexes," which does not serve organizations or society and is now, in fact, limiting our progress as a whole. This kind of conversation also avoids a critical reality: when made self-aware, both women and men **can change**. This is good news to those who are willing to embrace change and evolve. *This is not about "fixing" our self; it is about learning and growing to reach more of our true potential.*

In fact, our inclination to cling to stereotypical role-playing models based on gender is at the heart of many of our leadership woes. For example, men limit their leadership ability by clinging to the belief that they must be stoic and repress their sense of empathy and connection to others. This type of behavior limits heart engagement and the ability to inspire others. There is new research demonstrating that men indeed show signs in early childhood development and into adulthood that they have equal ability to access empathy. Women who believe the "woman's place" is to remain in the background are not very likely to assert themselves when needed, or to voice their authentic opinion without fear of rejection. Needless to say, the ability to navigate change in organizational culture is limited by this type of behavior on the part of the leader. Both of these socially perpetuated behaviors tend to be unconsciously conditioned in us as children, and there is now new, compelling research to support this claim.

BEHAVIORAL MEMORY IN OUR CELLS

We now know that memory is stored in our body at a cellular level until "updated" and released. It is stored in the "subconscious mind" of our self. If done with conscious intention, this "reprogramming" can be more readily accessed. Do not underestimate the power of conscious choice to implement change. One of the most important steps to achieving this shift is holding an open mind and having the courage to willingly change. Our brain is "Neuroplastic," meaning it can rewire and change itself to adapt to mental, emotional, and environmental change. Adult learning is optimal when we approach new information with an open mind. This is what growth and innovation is all about—thinking differently.

In fact, I have known men in my personal life, or as clients, who have expressed the desire to behave more empathetically but fear a negative social response to their exhibition of "female" behavior. Denial is a strong psychological self-defense mechanism. Stop and think about the saying "big boys don't cry," as if feelings and emotions are only female human characteristics, and/or the characteristics of a weak baby. If this were true, then why are male bodies biologically designed with the ability to feel and cry? This rejection of natural human emotion is a part of the problem and is a socialized response, not "Nature" at work. Hopefully, the new research on "The Science of Feelings" will broaden the conversation on this topic of emotion. Because we reject our feelings, we are prone to close our minds when they are provoked becoming perceptually blind to the cognitive dissonance that results in our behaviors. We continue to say, "women are empathetic" and "men are command-control," even when we witness the opposite at times within the context of our lives. I have encountered these contradictions on many occasions. I've experienced empathetic men and command-control women. I've been a command-control woman in my own journey. Likewise, I've been able to re-embrace my empathetic heart as I've become more self-aware. The point is, we can break stereotyping more effectively when we all stop stereotyping men and women.

When men are stereotyped as being one way, this is just as much a barrier to leadership style change as promoting that women are "nice but incompetent." It would serve leaders—no, human beings—better to allow individuals to develop as unique people, whether male or female. Allowing people's minds to open and choose the behavior characteristics that work best for them personally and for the culture of their organizations is a giant leap forward. Self-awareness combined with neuroplasticity of the brain allows for limitations to be cast aside so that the authenticity of the individual can be embraced whole-heartedly. In doing so, and as an added benefit, one is more likely to be able to tap into one's true potential and life purpose.

The leadership advantage will belong to the one who is best equipped to be self-aware enough to adapt to change, tap into their inner genius, and relate to and inspire the best in people in real time—in the present moment as needed—and to align their behavior in their authentic personality style. This authentic style taps into one's purpose and passion. As long as a person, whether man or woman, continues to buy into the outdated information that somehow people's social behavior is prepackaged, homogeneous, and based on gender, he or she will remain stuck and ineffective. And "business as usual" will continue. We all have room to grow regardless of gender or IQ levels. Based on my personal experience within the context of the medical profession and on conclusions drawn from science, I believe that organizations should expand their definition of effective leadership based upon the context and the desired, intentional corporate culture.

We have a choice, and we can be proactive with everything from our confidence to how we see ourselves as leaders. These are the topics I will address in the following chapters. It is our lack of brain awareness that contributes to this dilemma of inauthenticity. And it is imperative that we begin to understand how our own brain functions. Brain awareness can help us uproot our outdated beliefs and "plant a new tree," as contemplated by the Chinese proverb that opens this chapter. With that, we will leave this discussion and embark upon new ways to gain a better understanding of our amazing brain.

Key Points

- The root of much of our inauthentic behavior and personality as leaders is molded by our culture; these assumptions are then wired into our minds by our "storytelling" brain.

- Research shows that it is ***the meaning we assign*** *to our thoughts, feelings, and experiences that matters to the quality of our decisions, the actions we take, and our lives.*

- There is strength in a diversity of leadership styles, and these styles are accessible via increasing self-awareness through personal development/brain awareness.

- Nurture (environment) can over-ride Nature (physical sex) when it comes to behavior and cognitive development.

- The danger in rooting gender myths in biology is that this implies that these differences are "hardwired" and unchangeable.

- Stereotypical behavioral forces are not rooted in biology; *they are rooted in culture.*

- "Survival of the Fittest" is a social paradigm that can be evolved with intention. It is not objective nor is it biologically "hardwired"; it is subjective. Cooperation and collaboration can be viewed as critical aspects of survival for the "whole of life."

- *The integration of strength and gentleness, individualism and community, and EQ/IQ balance are traits that are accessible to all human beings regardless of gender and are needed for resilient, visionary, and effective 21ˢᵗ century leadership—regardless of gender.*

- Men are capable of developing empathy and women are capable of developing assertiveness; neither gender has a corner on particular behavior traits.

- Optimal creativity has been found to be associated with teams that are balanced and diversified in gender and abilities.

Reflect: Inquiring Mind

1. If we are assigning meaning to our situations and circumstances that occur, how can this contribute to creating "self-fulfilling prophecy"?

2. How can effective situation-based leadership styles increase the ability of organizations to respond to changing environments?

3. How do empathy, effective emotional self-management, and present moment awareness to the problem at hand contribute to a leader's ability to implement his or her strategic vision?

4. Research findings have shown that the *meaning* we assign to our situations and circumstances (that is, our perceptions about them or "how" we see them) wire our brain, and thus create our "reality" (the way that we "think life is"), which powerfully impacts our resulting behavior. Hence, the conclusions we form that determine actions taken and resulting behavior are not objective; they are subjective.

5. Why do you think that many men and women continue to ignore objective research data regarding gender and cognitive

development, which reveal that behavior is not "hard-wired" and is influenced by life experience and culture?

6. How could the ability to "NeuroReIvent" yourself purposefully support you in accelerating and elevating your leadership effectiveness?

Envision Possibilities

1. What if you could learn to navigate your emotional landscape as easily and as effectively as you navigate your intellectual landscape? What would this look like and how would it change the "reality" of your life?

2. What would the workplace look like if there was a climate of harmony instead of the overly competitive atmosphere that exists in most organizational cultures? Imagine how this would contribute to employee engagement and productivity. See this in your mind's eye so as to gain insights into how to use this option to problem solve and find a solution to talent retention challenges.

3. How would reducing the "Battle of the Sexes" redirect energy toward leadership and organizational effectiveness and employee engagement? What would this look like from the leader's perspective all the way down to the front line employee's perspective?

CHAPTER THREE

LEADING WITH
THE BRAIN IN MIND

The hemispheres need to co-operate, but I believe they are in fact involved in a sort of power struggle, and that this explains many aspects of contemporary Western culture"

— Iain McGilchrist, Psychiatrist and author of
*The Master and his Emissary: The Divided Brain
and the Making of the Western World*

EXPANDING VISION IN OUR MIND'S EYE

Before you can begin to "Lead With the Brain in Mind," you will need to have a working knowledge of how to optimally operate your brain's capacity for attention with awareness. Your brain contains billions and trillions of cells, according to the general consensus of brain researchers. The practical implication is that it is an intricate and complex organ. It serves as the mechanism by which you form your identity and make sense of the world as it relates to YOU. *Your sense of self, which I will address in this chapter, is the center of your life experience and attention;* this is the orientation from which one's "survival instincts" and fear of change engage life experiences. This chapter is a foundational overview for understanding how to begin taking back the steering wheel of your mind.

Conscious awareness of this material is critical to being empowered to make desired changes in present behaviors.

I also want to state up front that, on the surface, it may seem as if the various informational sections in this chapter are unrelated to each other. However, this is definitely not the case. For example, one may initially wonder how our identity is connected to triggering the "Fight, Flight, Freeze" response. One of the reasons mental agility is so much of a challenge is that we have tended to think only in a linear, disconnected sequence. We don't slow down enough to take in seemingly disparate pieces of information so that we can see their connections to the whole. Innovation requires this skill development, which is essentially a dance between our "big picture" right-brain and our linearly processing tactical left-brain. This weaving together of the parts of the whole, which you may not see routinely, provides a richer and deeper understanding of the overall context. This is also an exercise for your brain that helps to make you a more adaptable 21st century leader. To use a metaphor from the classic Sherlock Holmes novels, most people are like Dr. Watson, an inductive thinker who tends toward piecemeal logic and generalization. The 21st century thinker is a more deductive type of thinker, like Sherlock, who first synthesizes and deduces seemingly disparate broad pieces of information and then connects them to form a more specific conclusion. This process activates collaboration between both brain hemispheres in the educational, creative, and problem-solving process. It would be important to keep this collaborative process in mind as you read this chapter.

In order to get to the root of the current leadership challenge and improve performance, leaders must become aware of the *source* by asking the question, what is beneath the inability to execute one's skill sets and intentions in everyday terms? To make behavioral change easier, a leader must learn to see him or her self objectively and with compassion, instead of berating oneself or denying that growth is needed. To be able to do this, we need new tools that have practical application within the context of business and life. This chapter is devoted to sharing some scientific information in a colloquial way with business leaders like *you* so that you can begin to learn how to operate your brain optimally. That will allow you to effectively and with greater ease take your personal and professional growth to the next level and beyond.

Of course we use our brains, but we have been doing so without any real conscious intention because most of us lack any understanding of how the brain works. This is not cause for embarrassment; we have all been doing the best we can with the information that we had. Our lack of awareness of this crucial information accounts in large measure for why change and personal development can be so difficult and challenging. We now have an opportunity, however, to embrace an innovative way of thinking so that we can improve our personal and professional performance. By taking advantage of these new revelations, we can now expand our capacity to positively motivate ourselves and others, see the potential for growth and the opportunities that are available to us, and courageously navigate our rapidly changing environment with much greater ease.

Seeing Through a New Lens

Motivating yourself with an inner critic, which is associated with creating stress or fear of loss, is counterproductive in this brave new world of constant change with its need for adaptive leadership styles. Self-defensive behaviors that result from listening to our inner critic are typically distracting, waste time, cause stress, and drain our energy. In addition, ignoring the need to change your behavior is not going to make you a successful leader. The path to evolving and growing lies in learning new professional skill sets while, at the same time, learning how to integrate contextually, and with more positive emotion, our *personal growth*. Recall from the Introduction the impact that perception can have on how we view and respond to learning and development. This is not about "fixing yourself." It is about learning and growing to reach more of your true potential. Until now, we have been ignoring the importance of evolving our mindset.

Research has already demonstrated that the "brain on happiness" is more effective, smarter, and productive than a "brain on fear." Healthy optimism optimizes productivity. The ability to self-regulate one's behavior with self-awareness creates a leadership advantage. This is the basis of emotional intelligence. It increases one's confidence and likelihood of success. As a society, if we want people to be inspired and perform at their best, we need to shift our focus from fear to living and leading with purpose. Personal fulfillment also has become a meaningful goal for many people. This not only improves cognitive function and raises job satisfaction, but it supports better physical health, which can lead to a reduction in absenteeism and loss of employee productivity.

Thanks to neuroscience research, we can now engage our "logical" mind to realize that the neuroplasticity of the brain offers a way to accelerate much needed personal growth. Science also grounds your logical mind so that it can engage in this conversation without suspicion of a process that is too "touchy feely." Neuroplasticity allows us to engage our logical mind in this conversation of transformation and growth in a way that can help us to get out of our own way. In this new work environment, "soft-skills," which include emotional intelligence and people-skills, matter as much as the traditional hard skills. Science grounds these concepts into our everyday experience, which can be very important for "left-brain-dominant" Western cultures.

Neuroscientists do not understand everything about the brain, of course, and there is a constant expansion of information as it becomes available. Much of what I speak about is substantiated by current progressive research and theory, and some is empirical evidence drawn my own experience, from my clients, and from other resources. Remember, you don't need to have a degree in neuroscience or be able to recall brain anatomy to optimally program it for your own use. **You just need to understand** *how to operate* **your brain optimally so that you can be most effective at using its "Inner Technology."**

Eye Opening Research

Brain research shows that how we see the world and ourselves is a projection of the inner self-images that our minds create, including gender role images. It is not that these images are "good" or "bad"; the question is, however, are they currently serving you and our modern day society? If so, how? If not, why? Also, how do these images get into our minds in the first place? Is our current paradigm the most efficient and effective way of seeing the world and ourselves? By now, I have had many clients who have demonstrated that changing self-image changes behavioral responses. The way one perceives him or herself shifts. Our thinking can and does change. I've witnessed client responses to others, their ability to take risks, voice their opinion, or stand up for themselves as they evolve to more effective levels. From the perspective of my own experience, one really doesn't need science to make this connection between thinking differently and behavior change; it is generally intuitive.

Perhaps we should consider that our current model of how we tend to see life is actually limiting our health, wealth, relationships, and global ability to make a meaningful impact. *Recognizing* this negative impact *is* a form of new thinking or innovation. Holding limiting views of others or ourselves is not supporting us in achieving the business and life success or the fulfillment so many people crave. Changing our thinking is at the root of innovation and effective change leadership. Learning how to take full advantage of your "whole brain" in real time has practical, day-to-day application. Due to our perceptions regarding "gender limitations," we typically create a "Divided Brain" that keeps us from accessing the full spectrum of our potential talents. Tapping both of our brain hemispheres intentionally can help us to reconnect with our "Ideal Self" image to function and perform more effectively. In the final analysis, the way in which we think and feel about ourselves drives our performance, for better or worse.

Our brain has vast potential for creating "self-fulfilling prophecy." The trick is to create business and life "realities" that allow us to take leadership and society to a new level—to innovate and create more win-win sustainable models. This requires a new vision and the knowledge of how to retrain our brain to remove existing blind spots that limit our potential for growth. We haven't realized, until recently, how detrimental some of our business and social models (or ways of seeing the world), have programmed our views of self and our world in a way that constricts our true potential.

This represents a huge missing piece of the puzzle. This realization and its application have radically raised the quality of my life in every area. I have helped my clients to do the same, often with very positive results. Having awareness of how our brain "optimally operates" certainly can make a dramatic difference in our ability to change. Of course, we must be motivated to change. If we pay attention, it seems we have daily opportunities to find a reason to become motivated!

EPIGENETICS: YOUR GENES ARE *NOT* YOUR DESTINY

Very current research is showing that nurture often can trump nature due to the brain's ability to change itself based on one's thoughts, feelings, environment, and experiences. This field of biology is known as "Epigenetics" and is also related to this new idea of how perception changes our growth and experience of life. Based on biological reality, it is virtually impossible to say that our behavior is "hard-wired" by our genes. Environment has a profound effect on behavior, including gender role assignment. The new burgeoning field of epigenetics is adding to the brain neuroplasticity conversation and rendering the "hardwired" argument to explain behavior obsolete.

Epigenetics demonstrates that our genes are not our destiny. Our environments can change our gene expression, and these effects can even be transmitted to the next generation. *Epi*, in Greek, means "above or beyond." There are physiologic conditions that can turn genes on or off via molecules that can influence DNA expression. Thus, even if one has a genetic tendency, this does not mean it has to be expressed. Social norms influence our perceptual development. Likewise, epigenetics reveals that new thoughts, feelings, and behaviors can impact our gene pool going forward into the future, even through the next generation. The differentiator once again appears to be social context and environment, including nutrition.

Biological sex does not determine what behavioral changes are made—choices do. This certainly aligns with my own behavioral experiences of personality change. Over time, my personality has evolved traits traditionally attributed to both "male" and "female" leadership styles, and I continue to evolve my unique personality balance. Our personality is not static or limited to our biological sex.

Our DNA is like an extensive CD collection; just because you have a CD doesn't mean that you will play it, and just because you have a gene doesn't mean that it is turned on (expressed). Instead, the extent to which genes are expressed is strongly affected by the environment.

— Dr. Richard Davidson, author of
The Emotional Life of Your Brain

BELIEF: OUR BRAIN'S BLUEPRINT

We have not understood how this lack of brain awareness has caused us to unwittingly create situations, circumstances, and even a self-image that does not serve the highest good for ourselves as leaders—as human beings—or for society as a whole. What you believe about yourself can make or break you. Belief is the blueprint for your nervous system. "Belief," however, is tricky because it involves more than just "positive thinking." It involves feelings and "consciousness." "Belief" doesn't make it "true"; it just means YOU believe it to be true, so that your brain will cause you to **react and take action** based upon this belief. Hence, your belief contributes to your experience of "reality." This is how perception works.

For example, what you believe about your own ability can determine your willingness to take risks and develop new skills or behaviors. What you believe about others—their gender, race, culture, educational background—will influence how you respond to them consciously or unconsciously. Just because you believe the way you do, doesn't make something "true." Hence, particularly in our increasingly diverse workplace, our system of beliefs can support or hinder our leadership potential. Here is a question to consider: *Does what I believe improve my performance, relationships and well-being, and align with my stated values or not?* If not, you may want to consider shifting your belief.

BELIEF CONSTRUCTS PARADIGMS

New paradigms and constructs can at first feel intimidating, but once you retrain your brain to be able to stay open to new concepts and ideas, it gets easier with time. It's like learning to drive a car; at first it feels awkward, but then it becomes automatic over time. You have the capacity to innovate, probably beyond what you currently even imagine. For the sake of simplicity and to avoid confusion, I will mostly refer in this context to the physical organ of the brain, though it will appear that sometimes there is an interchangeability of usage with the word "Mind." Mind refers to "the process of the regulation of energy and information." "Brain" is a more commonly used word in most people's vocabulary, referring to the physical structure. And it is the tangible object that neuroscience can readily study.

If we want to get to the root of our dilemma regarding more effective performance, we must turn our attention to a deeper point of interest. *Research shows that, as we change our perception inside of our mind, we are better able to make the corresponding change in our outer environment.* This includes how we think of our self and *what we can be, do, and have.* We are currently struggling to create different results, but are using the same mindset that created our current dilemmas.

When it comes to paradigm shifting in particular, there will not be unanimous agreement. Recall that science and a multitude of people once **believed** the earth was flat and the center of our universe. We find past modes of thinking humorous at times; yet it seems history continues to repeat itself when it comes to embracing change. The following are a few reminders.

All truth passes through three stages. First, it is ridiculed. Second, it is violently opposed. Third, it is accepted as being self-evident.

— Arthur Schopenhauer,
German philosopher (1788–1860)

The telephone has too many shortcomings to be seriously considered a means to communication.

— Western Union (1876)

There is a world market for maybe five computers.

— IBM's Thomas Watson (1943)

What is "true" within cultures evolves over time. I was taught in medical school, in the early 1980s, that our brains could not grow new brain cells beyond approximately 20 years of age. This aligned with the old adage: "You can't teach an old dog new tricks." I doubted this as "science fact." Fortunately, given that we now know that what we believe about our brain's capability has such a huge impact on our "reality," my suspicions proved accurate. We had insufficient technology at the time to even make such a statement. Science evolves. Growth requires an open mind. Trust your own intuition as to what works for you. Trust your gut. *If we really want to innovate, we must be willing to look for new answers to old questions when we are not getting the results that evolve us upward and onward as a society.* The fact is, considering where our organizations and institutions are today, it is important to stop wasting time recycling old ideas that are not serving us and get "unstuck." This is true for both gender arguments and for the way in which we operate our institutions. Greatness is not a snapshot in time; evolution is required to stay truly "Great."

BASIC NEUROSCIENCE 101 AND HOW IT APPLIES TO YOU AS A LEADER

Leadership is a journey of self-discovery that includes personal and professional growth. In order to most effectively embrace this journey, we need to understand what is most powerfully impeding our development. Neuroscience now allows us to engage our logical mind in this process, instead of continuing to have it actually block us from expanding our vision of what we are capable of achieving. Science has shown that an overactive analytical left-brain can interfere with "insights" generated from the bigger picture, contextual right-brain hemisphere. Neuroscience allows us to more efficiently remove the blind spots that hold us back from reaching our true leadership potential. It allows us to more consciously engage *both reason and intuition/imagination*—**both brain hemispheres**—to accomplish this. Let us begin by examining some of our current paradigms.

Paradigm Filters

Currently, the predominant cultural belief is that we must view others as a threat instead of cooperating with others "in order to survive." We need to better understand how to reframe this often stress-provoking, unbalanced, "competitive" paradigm if we are to learn to collaborate with others.

The majority of people think that they are in control of their decisions. This is not totally accurate since 90–95% of what runs our life is out of conscious awareness for the vast majority of people. You read that correctly—90–95%! For the most part, only 5% is within our daily awareness. Stanford researcher, Fred Luskin, stated that we think 60,000 thoughts per day with 90% of them being repetitive—for better or for worse. These thoughts are typically a part of our 95% blind spot. Once we form a belief, it goes out of our consciousness and daily awareness, and the automatic response areas of our brain take over. This is why we need to intentionally develop greater self-awareness.

Our brain takes what we repetitively focus on or experience with great emotion and wires these responses for future use so that we won't need to consciously think about what to do when a similar situation occurs. We are limited as to how much we can focus on at one time with our 5% conscious mind. This is the brain's way of being efficient; your nervous system will automatically react for you before you have time to "think about" your choices, once it wires a choice into the subconscious mind. **The key to accessing the 95% that you are not aware of is through increasing self-awareness**—a pivotal insight for leaders who want to grow and evolve. This is the starting point for conscious behavior change with less time and effort. Once we make ourselves aware of old patterns and change them, a domino effect can change other unproductive behaviors so that ultimately, these new patterns become our automatic behaviors. This is how we become more effective without having to "think" about it. The new behaviors will be your new habits once they enter into your subconscious mind. The more you practice, the easier it will become—much like riding a bike or driving a car.

Vertical Brain Evolution

The **physical brain** itself has undergone three vertical levels of evolution in its development, in addition to the horizontal plane of the "left and right-brain" structure (see the following diagram). These levels illustrate our evolving path to becoming more self-aware.

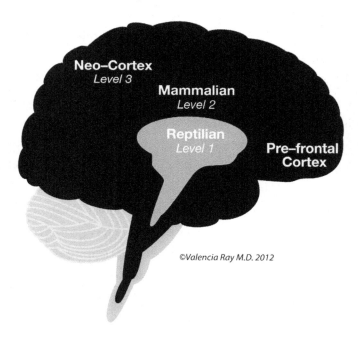

©Valencia Ray M.D. 2012

Level 1, the "Reptilian Brain," is concerned with keeping us alive and with our homeostasis; it is instinctual. Level 2, our Mammalian Brain (where you will find the often referred to "Limbic System"), for the practical purposes of this discussion, is our "social and emotional" brain. At this point in time, Level 1 and Level 2 are where most people spend most of their awareness. These two areas are associated with the paradigm of "fear and competition" because of the way we have constructed our social paradigm (The "Survival of the Fittest" model). This is our "Survival Brain." When we don't know how to skillfully access the next level (the neo-cortex, which is Level 3), we spend our lives comparing ourselves to others, in judgment of others, and on high alert for threat; we stay stuck in "Fight, Flight or Freeze." This is the source of the epidemic stress and overwhelm we witness all around us. According to brain development theory, the *prefrontal area* of the Level 3 neo-cortex is the area I call our "Thrival Brain". It is located within the neo-Cortex and is referred to as our "Crowning Glory." It is the Seat of Self-Awareness. It is the "Executive Brain." When we learn how to skillfully access this level of our brain with intent to change our behavior, we can intercept the automatic responses of stress and competition. We can speak our truth with greater calm and security. We can better manage healthy boundaries so that we can express our own purpose more freely. We can be truly productive and intentional, not simply "busy." We can access greater creativity and empathy and develop a more expansive vision for our business and life. We can live a more whole and integrated life.

This information is presented with the purpose of informing you of these distinctions so that you can be aware that you need to learn to purposely access your Level 3 Thrival brain in order to become a more effective, engaging leader who walks his or her talk with consistency. Without doing this, you are subject to continue on whatever trajectories you have been on with very little likelihood of sustainable change. Metaphorically, you are likely to live and die, "stuck" in the Level 1 and 2 areas of your brain. The lack of understanding of this concept is at the heart of why change is so difficult and challenging for most of humanity. Later in this book, I will share practice exercises that can help you better access your Level 3 brain.

Insight research shows that areas of the neo-cortex are involved in the "aha" process. It is the arena for imagining new possibilities. It can then be combined with our old memories (what we already "know") and the "logic" of our conscious mind to arrive at a new innovation on an old concept. This is how we gain creative insight. It can be a new invention or, more commonly, an innovation on an existing concept. ***Creativity is a process that involves our whole brain and includes both hemispheres.*** Our memories and meanings work collaboratively with the other phases of minds. Our memories can make available old patterns that can be used to ground a new idea in a present reality. Or, these same memories can keep us stuck, depending on our level of self-awareness.

How does "cellular memory" work? When we hear an old song and it stirs up our emotion and memories or images, or if someone does something that provokes anger and causes an exaggerated response from us that is out of context to the present moment, it is our cellular memory that is responsible for our "Re-ACTion." We re-enact the original painful or joyful meaning physiologically. This explains the source of emotional over-reactivity that is out of context in the present moment. The response is tied to old repressed feelings that were never resolved and continue to haunt us, sometimes at very inopportune moments. Our brain functions as a "meaning assigning machine" and it is subjective! It is for this reason that conscious, intelligent management of our emotions can be so helpful. This energy of feelings and their meaning are stored in our body's subconscious mind until we become conscious of how to move them out, and then do so. The meaning we habitually assign to situations can influence our leadership vision and capacity for innovation.

If we do not begin to realize that *we assign meaning to our situations and circumstances based on our old patterns of memory,* we are not likely to break self-sabotaging patterns of habitual thought. We will only continue to talk about innovation because we will not be able to access our genius and take whatever action is necessary to actually manifest our creative ideas and paradigms for business development and growth.

This dance between old concepts and new insight is the source of innovative ideas. We take new concepts and develop tangible, physical ways to bring the new idea into physical form. This is the creative process that births innovative business ideas into the world. We can access and accelerate this ability by learning how to intentionally engage our right-brain via activities such as reflection, playfulness, artistic endeavors (such as painting and drawing without rigid structure), relaxation, and meditation. You need to be aware that if you don't intentionally respect and access your right-brain hemisphere, your logic can keep you stuck on what you "already know." **You will tend to look only into the existing file cabinet of your mind to stay in your comfort zone, with its false sense of "predictability."** In reality, only the sun rising and setting is truly predictable on a daily basis. You are most effective when you take advantage of the integrated effort between all areas of your mind and tap your Level Three brain on purpose in order to create skillfully.

SCRIPTING YOUR OWN AUTOBIOGRAPHY AND THE MEANING OF LIFE

As mentioned previously, science reveals that we are constantly assigning meanings to our lives and then we believe that these meanings are "just the way life is." These meanings become our "script." This includes not only what happens to us, but it is also how we form "Who we think we are"—our "Autobiographical Memory." *Our identity is the story we tell our self about our self.*

All the world's a stage and all the men and women merely players.

— Shakespeare

Your sense of self-image and self-esteem are at center stage of what runs your life experience. Your right and left-brain hemispheres work as a team to form your self-image, and hence your "ego-self" structure—your "Mental Me." Your autobiographical memory narrative forms and maintains or changes your ego construct. Your conscious mind connects this ego construct to the actions you take in the external world. Ego means "I" in Latin. Ego is not "bad"; it is how we define our human self. It is our personality. Built right into the word "personality" is the root word "persona," which means, "Mask." It is a mental construction, formed by your perceptions and assumptions about life and your relation to it.

Ego also includes our belief about our self-worth—what we think we can be, do, or have. It is the center of our mental "universe," meaning that how we approach others and our lives will be heavily determined by how we see ourselves first. The trick here again is to be able to be honest with your self and allow your subconscious beliefs, carried within the ego self, to surface. Remember, we all have "cellular memory." Our sense of identity profoundly affects our confidence and ability to communicate. If we are not aware of how we form our sense of identity, we will typically "re-act" our old childhood and prior dramas. This will impact our ability as a leader to have an open mind and see our team members' potential clearly. It determines if we will be defensive and controlling or if we have sufficient confidence in ourselves to allow others to articulate their ideas in the conversation. Needless to say, engagement of others hinges upon our ability as a leader to inspire and confidently embrace and lead change. Our sense of identity is at the core of leadership success or failure. When we understand how we form our identity, we can learn how to change it if it no longer works for us.

Consider the following example. If you are a woman who grew up in a household where the boys were encouraged to speak up while the girls were silenced, you may operate from one of two patterns when challenged. On the one hand, you may have an identity that says, "I am not valued." You may be prone to feeling intimidated when communicating your vision to a group of men and therefore to withhold your opinion. In short, you may find yourself fearing rejection.

On the other hand, if your coping personality as a child was to assert yourself more aggressively in order to get attention, you may tend to push your views on those same men and be unreceptive to their viewpoints. Your sense of identity may be, "I am a fighter." How we define our identity drives our responses within all of our relationships. Yet, when we learn how to evolve those "parts" of our self that are narrowly defined and stuck in time from our past, we can become more present in the moment and respond appropriately instead of reactively. Be consistently mindful of the words used behind, *"I am _____"* because you are sending a pattern to your brain's neurons (cells) that will wire your future identity perceptions. This language, spoken about ourselves, contributes to how the ego forms and re-forms.

As you learn to realize that you are "making up the meaning," it can become easier to change your "story line." Changing your storyline essentially is what evolving is all about. Thoughts about what happened (i.e., our story), create corresponding feelings within our body. But this is a subjective process, and it can be reframed. It is very empowering to know that "YOU" are not your thoughts. You can change the "ego structure" of your Mental Me if it no longer serves you. As articulated in some neuroscience circles,

Don't believe everything you think.

The voice of our inner critic is really a tape of the ego and our fearful self-images of autobiographical memory—a part of those 60,000 thoughts per day that are repetitive. The inner critic can be retrained to be a supportive voice of encouragement instead of one that provokes stress and discomfort. I know because I've done it. This is the journey to self-acceptance and compassion, which is so very powerful and supportive to becoming a more engaging leader. We need to develop a healthier "Intrapersonal Relationship" by being willing to invest more time in reflection, getting to know our purpose and True Self. Your critical voice can be converted to one that simply intuitively reminds you to do the things necessary to reach your goal instead of berating and pushing you to react.

A short read that provides a cogent real-life example can be found in the book, *My Stroke of Insight*, written by Harvard trained neuroscientist, Dr. Jill Bolte-Taylor. She experienced a stroke while in her 30s that temporary knocked out her left-brain self-image ego capacity. Her narrative explains how she literally lost her sense of everyday individuality and identity. Without her ego, she felt that she had lost her ability to navigate effectively as an individual within our 3D world. She could not even take the action required to save her own life because she was so "blissed out."

The point is that we need our ego brain constructs to survive as human beings on this earth and to make sense of the world around us. The problem is not the ego construct; the problem is how we program this ego construct. For most people, the ego is inflexible and full of self-doubt and competitiveness to a fault. We have trained it to fear feelings and live in denial. We have the ability to develop higher functioning and productive ego identity constructs when we become self-aware of this ability.

In the beginning phases, learning to "retrain your brain" (like learning to drive a car) may feel awkward. Yet once you become clear about what leadership gaps you need to refine and what strengths you need to evolve, applying these lessons becomes second nature—just like driving a car. This allows us to live with greater ease and less struggle because we have trained our brain in a way that makes life more meaningful, and we can feel more confident and capable as a leader. Your brain can either support your growth or keep you stuck; you have the freedom to choose.

It is our fear of facing old cellular memories and our resistance to seeing life differently that hinders our ability to eliminate the blind spots that hold back our performance. The more we learn how to skillfully manage our feelings and emotions, the faster transformation will occur. We will be able to actually apply our emotional intelligence skill sets with consistency. As Harvard business professor and change expert John Kotter noted:

Behavior change happens mostly by speaking to people's feelings.

He then adds:

In highly successful change efforts, people find ways to help... see the problems or solutions in ways that influence emotions, not just thought.

Our fear of our feelings is equivalent to the childhood paradigm of "fear of the boogeyman under the bed." It is an illusion and unnecessary; yet, it has the physiologic power to create fear and inertia. Research shows that "how" we perceive pain or fear causes the brain to "act as if" it is "Reality." I know this to be true from experience. Since I have "made friends with my feelings," my capacity for embracing change skillfully and getting out of my comfort zone far exceeds anything I could have ever imagined just a decade ago. Taken to the extreme, some people avoid promotions for fear of failing. Feelings like these can even impact the workplace. Not to attempt something new is a sure way not to succeed. Also, when we tell our self that we don't fit in or belong, or when we fear rejection, our actions will tend to follow our thoughts and feelings. We thus might avoid social connection to those by whom we feel intimidated, or those who are, at times, in positions of authority to support our promotion. We often create self-fulfilling prophecy without realizing it.

When we become more self-aware of how to masterfully examine our thoughts, feelings, and beliefs, we can more easily update our thinking to adapt to new changes in our environment much more quickly. We stop wasting time living in denial and fearing change. We no longer stand by and watch other companies in our niche take our market share and run over us. This "brain awareness" capacity is imperative to becoming a more effective and engaging leader—for good.

Let us now examine the science of feeling since it is a critical concept for authentic and effective leadership.

THE SCIENCE OF FEELINGS

The science of feelings is now being reported—thankfully. Feelings are an important component of forming beliefs and taking action on our perceptions. If we do not become self-aware of how to manage our feelings with intention, they will hijack us before our logical minds have a chance to be engaged in the first place. Remember, our perception and the meaning of our feelings are housed in the subconscious memory and until we know how to access them with more conscious awareness, we will continue to act robotically.

Feelings play a very important role in "Courageous Conversations." In fact, if you fear your feelings, you will have very little courage to face a difficult conversation. Our tendency to shame our feelings accounts for why implicit communication problems are so prevalent in organizations of all sizes. *It is our lack of skillful self-management of feelings that is also at the root of blame and refusal to deal with the mistakes associated with ordinary learning curves.*

I realized long ago that my feelings often trumped my logical mind. "Making friends" with my feelings has given me much more self-control and inner peace of mind. It has also improved my empathy and ability to connect with others. But before we go on, let's review the "linearized" process for creating belief. The role that feelings play in forming our belief is described below. It is the glue that makes belief and memory stick. This is really an integrated, complex process. What follows is a way to simplify and understand it practically.

Thought, emotion, and feeling work together to form our "belief." It is critical to understand how we form beliefs if you desire to change yours. **Beliefs dictate our actions.** Emotion can be defined as the perception of love or fear, "good or bad," "like or dislike." It is based on how we see or judge the situation. Emotion forms the basis of our perception about what we are witnessing or experiencing. It is "Energy in Motion" or thought energized. It *moves* us. It is the meaning we assign to what we think or see that creates the perceptual trigger that **qualifies** or colors the subsequent feeling (sensations) and ultimately the *action taken*. Feeling, on the other hand, is "how" you feel in your body. It defines your "state of mind" or your "state of being." Joy, grief, happiness, gratitude are descriptors for feelings:

Thought + Emotion (Quality of Perception) = Feelings
Feelings => Beliefs => Actions

You take action based on your belief at the moment, but of course, this can change. Feelings energize our actions; it is the fuel. This is the reason that passion is so powerful in driving change. It is that invisible force that underlies how we "Be," as in how we *are* in the world. Feelings determine our "state of mind"—*the state of our mind.*

For example, if you see or *think* "dog" and are afraid of dogs (negative emotion and feeling/belief that you will be harmed—a moving away), you will have a different emotional response and feeling response than if you love dogs (positive emotion and feeling/belief that you are safe—a moving toward). This formula is a simplified version of how to think about the process that occurs in a small fraction of a second.

It is a cascading process that is linear at times and circular at times. Once we linearly wire our brain via this construct, the subconscious feeling can provoke the original thought or memory and, at times, create even a mental image of the original circumstance. This is how we form cellular memory and get stuck in "loops." We think and feel; we feel and think— then round and round we go if we do not understand how to break the cycle. When you fixate your attention on something, it expands in your awareness. As you can tell, this is distracting. Instead of being focused on the situation in front of you, you may ruminate about what was done or should have been done rather than acting appropriately *now.* This drains time, energy, and resources. It can also unnecessarily hinder future choices. Being able to live in the present moment certainly has its benefits.

Why are feelings so important in this formula? According to the Heart Math Institute in California (HeartMath.org), the magnetic energy of emotion/feeling is 5,000 times greater than that of thought alone. **This would account for why it can be so difficult to "think" your way out of a "belief."** A large part of belief is "feeling." We must learn how to release old stored feeling memory in an easier way that is acceptable to our rational mind. If we do not learn this, we will expend much of our mental energy repressing old feelings and avoid facing our present need to change. Engaging the logical, rational mind to understand the energy of thought, feeling, and emotion from a brain science perspective is a helpful place to begin. When the logical mind can engage in this process, it can actually dampen the reactive fight-flight-freeze response. It is important to reconcile our fear of feelings in order to sustainably apply our emotional intelligence skills. It is one thing to know *about* empathy, social awareness, and happiness theory; it is another thing to *apply* it.

To know and not to do is not to know.

— Chinese Proverb

We have been getting in our own way by not understanding how our brain operates to optimally produce results. Hence, we have been directing our brain in ways that are less useful and do not serve us well. Focusing on fear and negativity hinders IQ, clarity, and emotional intelligence. It damages our well-being, reduces team member engagement and productivity, and leads to unhappiness. There are many reasons for unlearning our less than ideal behavioral patterns. Happiness research has already connected the outcome of improved emotional intelligence application when one is in a place of emotional equanimity instead of turmoil.

Simply taking emotional intelligence (EI) skills seminars without addressing your own inner emotional landscape leads to self-deception about your own EI. It is challenging to be empathetic and inspiring to others when your own feelings are repressed and ignored. Remember, people can "feel your vibe." You may recall the old adage, "You can run but you cannot hide." Apparently, people are becoming more intuitive about this. They can sense inauthenticity like never before. The science of feeling is arriving just in time to help evolve our leadership style and avoid crisis.

The dominant question now is: *Do you truly feel comfortable with yourself enough to recognize that there's still room to grow as a person and as a leader, no matter where you are situated currently?* It is only when we *assign* the belief (remember, we are programming "meaning" and context into our brain) that something is wrong or deficient in us that we are led to pretend that we have it all together; sometimes even feeling like a "fake." No one has everything in perfect order 24/7; that is just not real life. The problem is that, as a culture and society, we have created a widely accepted perception that needing to "grow" is synonymous with being "bad" or "not good enough," thus provoking negative feelings. This is a false and limiting belief. The work place is a perfect venue in which to "self-actualize," considering that it is in the workplace that we develop our skill sets and will face challenging relationships.

Our inner ego image evolves over our lifetime as we expand our vision for our self. Wherever you are is just where you are today. It is time to create a new paradigm about what "personal growth" means. The "real you" is so much more than this current episode of your life. Our lives are an evolving adventure movie and not a still frame in time. As a leader, you will be better able to see your own blind spots when you truly understand this. Again:

> *The curious paradox is that when I accept*
> *myself just as I am, then I can change.*
>
> — Carl Rogers

When we understand that our brain creates our life's "storyline" based on *how we look* (subjective assumption) at our situation, circumstances, and the people around us, we can question these assumptions and choose better conclusions. You are the "Director" of your life story. After all, it's not **what** happens to you as much as it is ***the meaning you assign*** to what happens to you that determines the outcome of your life. When we lack an understanding of how we negatively wire our brains, we feel helpless and stuck. We keep focusing our attention on what we DON'T want, which is certainly not the way to create what you DO want. As humanity, we have done the best we can with what we knew to be true; now we need to deepen our knowledge and take ourselves to a new level of being. This concept of the role of self-identity and how it applies to business and leadership will be discussed in greater detail in chapter five. For now, it is helpful to realize that we can adjust our personality to align with our authentic values and goals when we realize how and are motivated to do so.

At this point, the most important lesson is to recognize that the brain works through the focus of *attention* coupled with the quality of feelings that you hold. Your focus of attention will give rise to your meaning of the event. Feelings affect your *intention* and energy level. Have you ever walked into a room and "*felt* its vibe," emanating from the people there? Feelings are important. We are much more likely to succeed with change when we have clarity and heart-engagement in an enthusiastic way, than when we are too busy to reflect on clarity and values and are in a constant state of worry or fear. This is not rocket science.

In the next chapter, I will address some practical applications of this information regarding (a) how it looks theoretically when we are accessing left-brain versus right-brain aspects (horizontal anatomy) and, (b) how showing up in the different "3 Levels" of brain evolution (vertical anatomy) plays out. Neuroplasticity demonstrates that we can rewire our brain, but we need to understand the basic information regarding how each hemisphere and level of "brain awareness" influences behavior so that we can be more aware of how to change intentionally. The "Battle of the Sexes" reflects a current lack of understanding of our broader potential to intentionally tap into aspects of our mental and emotional capacity that is already available to us. If we want to become an engaging, effective leader, we need to examine more deeply how we direct our brain hemispheres in ways that create our leadership experience. In doing so, we can become more skillful at directing our attention and intention, two factors that contribute profoundly to the root of our performance and are especially crucial to resiliency and adaptability.

Key Points

- **Definition of Terms for Levels of Brain**:
  1. Level 1 – Reptilian Brain: It is concerned with keeping us alive and with our homeostasis; it is instinctual.
  2. Level 2 – Mammalian Brain: Social and emotional brain (Limbic)
  3. Level 3 – Thrival Brain: It is formally known as the neo-cortex and includes the prefrontal cortex. When we understand how to "optimally operate" our brain and intentionally access more of our Thrival Brain with purpose, we can quiet the Survival Brain

levels [Levels 1 and 2 combined] and better connect emotionally with our teams because we have greater clarity, confidence, peace of mind, and have elevated our decision making and strategies.

- *Your sense of self, which I addressed in this chapter, is the center of your life experience and attention*; this is the orientation from which one's "survival instincts" and fear of change engage life experiences.

- *"Optimally operating"* your amazing brain requires understanding the basic inner technology (not detailed neuroanatomy) of the way your brain uses thought, feelings, perception (emotion), and memories to determine the actions that you will take—all based on your "Story-telling Brain."

- In this new work environment, "soft-skills," which include emotional intelligence and people-skills, matter as much as the traditional hard skills.

- Our current model of how we tend to see life is actually limiting our health, wealth, relationships, and global ability to make a meaningful impact.

- Tapping both of our brain hemispheres intentionally can help us to reconnect with our "Ideal Self" image to function and perform more effectively. In the final analysis, the way in which we think and feel about our self drives our performance, for better or worse.

- When we learn how to skillfully access the neo-cortex of our brain (Level 3) with intention to change our behavior, we can intercept the automatic responses of our Mammalian (Level 2) and Reptilian (Level 1) Brain.

- Our brains have vast potential for creating "self-fulfilling prophecy."

- If we do not become self-aware of how to manage our feelings with intention, they will hijack us before our logical minds have a chance to be engaged in the first place.

- Epigenetics demonstrates that our genes are not our destiny.

- Beliefs construct paradigms; they are the blueprint for how your nervous system filters your worldview.

- Biological sex is not what determines which behavior changes are made—choices do.

- *Our identity is the story we tell our self about our self.*

- Don't believe everything that you think—reflect intuitively instead of only thinking inductively or literally. Critical thinking skill requires both.

- Feeling influences thoughts and decision making:

  Thought + Emotion (Quality of Perception) = Feelings;
  then, Feelings => Beliefs => Actions

- It is critical to realize that the brain works by focusing attention and the *feelings of intention* (whether the intention is conscious and self-aware or not) to determine what is important "to YOU." This determines the "reality" that you experience. Guard your mind and heart's focus of attention and intention mindfully.

Reflect: Inquiring Mind

In order to get to the root of the current leadership challenge to improve performance, leaders must become aware of the *source* by asking these questions:

1. What is beneath your inability to execute your skill sets and intentions in everyday terms? How could you benefit from

this ability to be more mentally agile and see beyond the immediate surface? Can this ability help you with both inductive and deductive reasoning ability in the midst of change?

2. Does "Who you think you are" evolve? Is your self-image the same now as it was when you were twelve? Twenty-five? Forty? Have you thought about how powerful it could be if you could update the current version of *"Who do you think you are?"* with clarity and intention—proactively?

3. What do you think about the idea that "You are not your thoughts"?

4. How does it change your perspective to know that "Your genes are not your destiny"?

5. How would helping your team develop a clear and compelling mental vision, including clarity in regard to purpose, passion, and values, support implementation of your strategic plan?

Envision Possibilities

1. What does your "Ideal Future Self" look, feel, and act like? Let your imagination expand the vision for your life.

2. Who are the characters and what are their roles in your Mental Rehearsal of this Ideal Self. Embellish this "Theater of the Mind" with as much five-sensory detail as possible. You should "feel it."

3. How would this new "YOU" be able to inspire team trust, reduce fear of conflict, and increase accountability and commitment at the office? How will this improve your results? How could this help to achieve your ideal relationships in all parts of your life? See it in your Mind's Eye now.

CHAPTER FOUR

THE DIVIDED BRAIN AND THE BATTLE OF THE SEXES

Once the brain has a goal in mind, it tunes the perceptual system to search the environment for relevant clues.

— Steven Sloman, cognitive scientist,
Brown University

THE POWER STRUGGLE THAT CAN LIMIT OUR POTENTIAL

Expanding the vision for our lives can be challenging when we do not understand how our brains seek to find what we already believe to be "true." It is uncanny how we only see what our perceptual system has already wired as "the way life is." This can lead to serious blind spots when we are not self-aware. Our brains will find the things that they considers relevant to prove we are "right" and virtually ignore the evidence that contradicts our current worldview. We have not understood until now just how literal the battle between our brain hemispheres, that keeps us locked in on our "known world," translates to our experience with the "Battle of the Sexes."

91

I began the last chapter with a quote from Dr. Iain McGilchrist's book *The Divided Brain*:

The hemispheres need to co-operate, but I believe they are in fact involved in a sort of power struggle, and that this explains many aspects of contemporary Western culture.

When I first read McGilchrist's book, I was taken with the fact that it appeared to validate, in a very thoughtful way, my own experience of the "power struggle" between my brain hemispheres and how this was playing out in my life. I intuitively knew that most of my resistance to change was coming from my left-brain. I knew that it was my "conscious mind" interfering, and its resistance to subconscious memories or to what was happening in the present moment was making me uncomfortable. I also came to realize that it was my cultivated ability not to need to "know" everything that allowed for insights and real connection to my sense of spirit self and to the whole of life. I began to comprehend that the less I lived "in my head" (metaphorically, the left-brain), the more I was able to reconnect to my heart and feelings (metaphorically, the right-brain). Accessing both sides of my brain and using my whole brain consciously was most powerful. This is a critical concept, because once the perceptual system has attuned itself to a pattern, it will continue to seek relevant clues within the environment that match what you have unwittingly wired your brain to "believe." This applies even to believing that one is essentially "left-brained" or "right-brained." You may have a preference or personality tendency, but you can access either side with intention and practice.

Admittedly, this was very uncomfortable at first. Indeed, years ago I did not have the advantage of "logically" understanding what I was experiencing. My logical left-brain kept giving me a hard time by stimulating feelings of fear of the "unknown." **Recall from chapter three that *both* hemispheres have a role in "feelings management."** Eventually, I began to trust my inner "knowing" and created a type of collaboration between my logical and intuitive mind. I now come from a place of pragmatism and believe that, if I cannot apply something to real life, it is a waste of time for me. What I've come to see is that:

$$1+1=5$$

By this I mean that, when I can create cooperation or internal collaboration between my brain hemispheres, my intelligences, including reasoning, increase on many levels. This is how I began to tap into my "multiple intelligences" instead of only relying on my intellect for so-called "proven facts." As previously stated, when it comes to new discoveries, what we know as true today can be proven false tomorrow.

IT TAKES TWO TO TANGO

We need a working understanding of how the differences between our brain hemispheres are manifest in the physical, everyday world as this relates to leadership performance. To help us begin this process, I will address two points:

1. the known functions and interrelatedness of the brain hemispheres in creating our experience, and

2. the role of intention (feeling) and attention (focus) in creating experience and performance. This point will be developed further on in the section on "**Neuroimaging and Behavior**."

Of course, much more could be covered. However, the intent of this book is to address only the basics regarding the question: *Can we retrain our brains to become more effective leaders, regardless of gender?*

INTERRELATEDNESS OF THE TWO BRAIN HEMISPHERES IN CREATING OUR EXPERIENCE

First, realize that your brain hemispheres are always participating on some level. Even though we historically have ignored the right-brain and treated it disdainfully, it still has contributed to our functioning. For example, as you will see in the Brain Hemisphere Behaviors chart presented further on, while the left-brain contributes to verbal expression, the right-brain contributes context, metaphor, and humor to language.

Much of what we know about the difference between our two brain hemispheres comes from "split brain" studies that were conducted in the 1960s. These studies involved operations that were performed on patients with intractable epilepsy as a last attempt to quell their seizures. The researchers in fact severed the bridge that connects the two hemispheres—the corpus callosum. Hence the name, "split brain." This allowed the researchers to present stimuli to just one hemisphere at a time. They discovered that the two hemispheres act independently and have two different processing styles. They act in complementary fashion to each other, yet they act differently.

The Brain Hemispheres Behaviors Chart presented later in this chapter is intended to provide a tangible (albeit theoretical in some ways) example of how the function of each brain hemisphere contributes to the behaviors that we demonstrate. What I have done is to separate the "dysfunctional" distinctions in an exaggerated, extreme way from the "functional" so that you can appreciate to some extent the "division of labor" within our brains. Another way of looking at this: too much left-brain leads to rigidity and too much right-brain leads to chaos. By learning how to develop collaboration between our brain hemispheres, we can integrate them more effectively, leading to greater mental agility that allows us to perform at our best. Of course, nothing is black and white, and there are many shades of gray.

I also want to make a couple of "non-traditional" distinctions about the brain hemispheres. The right-brain is the metaphor for the "heart"; it dominates the realm of our feelings and intuitions. It is the art side of life, and more deeply connected to our emotional brain. The left-brain is the metaphor for the "head." By "head," I mean the rational, logical, analytical, intellectual realm that often represses feeling unless one has skillful emotional self-awareness. It is the science side of life. Both sides contribute to the head and heart. We have two brain hemispheres for good reason. Two hemispheres really are better than one.

Of course, even when people deny their feelings, or suppress or repress them, these feelings continue to impact the human journey. Just because you deny your feelings does not mean they do not exist. Ignored feelings can create disease in your body and turbulence in your mind. They can also manifest at the most inopportune moments, as sometimes occurs when people who are otherwise controlled offer an explosive outburst. Overall, you can think of the left-brain as handling matters of our 3D external, physical experience and the right-brain as being in charge of the internal, spiritual, or invisible realm of our human experience. Skillful "NeuroReInvention" requires you to freely access the art and science aspects of your mind.

HOW DO HEAD AND HEART SUPPORT EACH OTHER?

Another metaphor that is crucial to this conversation relates to comparing behaviorally the right-brain aspect of ourselves and the left-brain aspect of ourselves. Our right-brain is receptive. It receives through reflection, and it allows us to receive by means such as listening, intuition, resting, imagining, and pondering the data for a big-picture context. It also provides inspiration for creativity. The right-brain sees the world through the lens of inter-relationship, whether between people or projects. Receptivity processes by "taking in." Think about our five senses; we receive stimuli from an external source. What we "take in" then becomes the basis for our intention regarding the "actions" that we take. Our perception is the meaning we assign to our sensory information. Our left-brain "puts out" and is concerned with taking action in the world by creating structure, linear process, or analyzing and separating facts. It sees the world in pieces. This attention to providing detailed steps and taking action animates and organizes the information "received" by the right-brain so that it can inform our actions. We take action (left-brain) based on what we believe we are receiving. We express into the world via the active force. *Hence, a person who operates his or her whole brain recognizes the importance of both receptivity and activity.* Making time to be receptive (engaging the qualities of our right-brain) before taking "massive action" (engaging the qualities of our left-brain) avoids wasting time, energy, and money. Both genders have the innate capacity to develop these brain functions. But the functions themselves are not based on gender. *Failing to understand this distinction only creates unnecessary confusion.* Men and women would benefit by tapping both sides of their brains based on their authentic personality style, and not gender conformity.

Women can choose to act with "active force" and assertively move out into the world, and men can choose to act with "receptive force" by receiving new ideas and connecting empathetically with others. It is not about gender; it is a matter of developing and exercising our ability to choose behaviors and responses that are unique to our own personalities. Different people will choose different personality behaviors with varying degrees of response in various circumstances, but this is not due to brain "hardwiring" and is not due to biological sex differences. Documented brain research increasingly demonstrates this fact. The more self-aware we become, the more able we are to choose wisely and within the context of where we are in the present moment. This is powerful as it relates to situational leadership.

The following is a simple, practical example of a metaphor for leadership:

As an effective leader, one needs to be able to guide and direct others as well as receive input. To illustrate this, I will use an example of a person who is driving a car and is lost. This person is busy ***driving, taking action***, but he or she is not clear about where they are headed and has not even determined the optimal route. Instead of stopping to ask for and ***receive*** directions or input, this person wastes over an hour before finally stumbling onto the correct street. He or she could have avoided wasted time, frustration (negative energy), and gas (money) simply by slowing down to receive support, get clarity (visioning the steps to the destination) and possibly better directions,—or at the very least, ***stopping to reflect*** about the map and thinking it through.

Some leaders act like the driver of the car. When one is too goal-oriented, taking action becomes ineffective as an optimal response. An individual may need to tap his or her receptivity, with self-awareness and wisdom as needed. In addition to creating stress for those involved, time, money, and resources are wasted. Stereotypical, inflexible behavior is a roadblock to visionary and engaging leadership, whether exhibited by a man or a woman.

Both genders have both brain hemispheres. Which side tends to dominate is highly influenced by conditioning and environment. *Nurture often trumps nature when it comes to adopting survival behaviors.* There are left-dominant females and right-dominant males. People tend to choose behaviors that align with the group culture they experienced as children. Of course, some women are naturally more left-brain and some men are naturally more right-brain in behavioral characteristics than others. Somehow, our culture continues to ignore these documented discrepancies in favor of the conflicting and stereotypical gender arguments. The path to self-mastery involves understanding how we write our brain scripts—how we construct the story line. We are more empowered when we become aware of what motivates us and what is authentic to our own life purpose. We have programmed our brain over time to an extreme degree because we have created an imbalanced paradigm of fear, competition, and scarcity, and thus we need predictability to feel safe. We therefore develop defense mechanisms. This then feeds into stereotypical role-playing. *At the root of survival-based, unconscious role-playing is fear in some form.*

For illustrative purposes, the following is a chart theoretically comparing the "division of labor" between our two brain hemispheres.

Brain Hemisphere Behaviors Chart

	Head	Heart
	Left-brain	Right-brain
Functional:	• Linear • Logic, facts, objectivity (+/-) • Linguistic • Structured, focused • Goal-oriented, singular • Critical • Separate from other; "self-identity" • Literal, rule-bound • Rational, physical/5 Senses • Active	• Non-linear, circular, simultaneous • Subjective • Context, reflection • Diffuse • Big-picture, complex • Non-judgmental • Connection, empathy, community • Metaphorical, humor/flexible • Intuitive, spiritual, feelings • Receptive

	Head	Heart
	Left-brain	Right-brain
Dysfunctional:	• Poor adaptability; lacks imagination • Uncomfortable with new ideas • Intimidates verbally, aggressive • Stuck on the tree, can't see the forest • Driven, stress-inciting behavior • Lacking empathy, disconnected • Insensitive, harsh, poor EQ • Needs predictability, inflexible, hierarchical • Rigid thinking; "see it to believe it - maybe"	• Scattered, lots of ideas, low action • Lacks caution • Passive voice, silent, daydreamer • Can't see the tree, no structure/process • Too laid back, procrastination • Excessive concern with feelings, too sensitive, timid • Poor boundaries, can't say "no"; inclusive to a fault • Not practical or grounded • Other worldly, spacey

SEEING THE BIG PICTURE

Notice that both men and women can operate on either side of the brain and in a variety of combinations. The brain is not divided strictly along gender lines. Women who "do too much" are really operating on the action-taking side of their brains, leaning toward over-activity. This is true whether they hold positions in the corporate world or do not work outside the home. A man who makes time to relax, rejuvenate, and to reflect on strategy and ideas is operating on the right side of his brain. Many women should take note of this for themselves. Women who focus on detail and process are operating on the left side of their brain, but also can access the big picture view of the right-brain. *People who lose their right-brain func-*

tionality experience a pathological narrowing of the focus of their attention because their left-brain focus is overactive. This will decrease creativity as well since the insight for new ideas comes generally through the right-brain's ability to see broadly and contextually.

Clearly, there are gifted female math and science students. What needs examination are the social pressures they experience in conforming to pre-conceived ideas of what is appropriately "female." This is culturally based. Some girls "dumb" themselves down in order to fit in socially. This has been offered to explain why the math and science skill set abilities of girls suddenly drop during and after the junior high school years in our educational system. (I recall struggling with this myself).

Limiting our discussion to historical paradigms that come from a place of competition between men and women, I read a report by the Barrett Values Centre, **"Understanding the Battle of the Sexes: The Effects of Gender on Leadership Style,"** written by Hannah Lee when researching this book. Without intent to criticize, the Centre's 2011 report exemplifies how we persist in asking the same old question: *How do men and women leaders differ along gender lines?* Instead, perhaps we should ask the following questions:

- *How can we effectively use the new brain science evidence demonstrating that environment and thinking influence brain perception and thus our behavior?*

- *How can we become leaders who are more self-aware instead of continuing to produce "self-fulfilling gender prophecy" beliefs that show up on empirical, self-reporting surveys?*

Recall the Steven Sloman quotation at the beginning of this chapter:

Once the brain has a goal in mind, it tunes the perceptual system to search the environment for relevant clues.

Once we have a goal in mind or something that we believe, we unconsciously begin to tune our perceptual system to look for and find what we expect, whether it is objective or not. For example, it is commonly stated that "women are more empathetic than men." Studies that report these types of findings collect their data from self-reported assessments. Self-evaluation is typically subjective. When more objective testing is done between men and women where physiologic response is measured, these differences in quantifying empathy are not reproduced. One study of this nature was conducted by Michalska, Kinzler, and Decety (2012) at The University of Chicago and reported in an article in the *Developmental Cognitive Neuroscience Journal* entitled, "Age-related Sex Differences in Explicit Measures of Empathy Do Not Predict Brain Responses Across Childhood and Adolescence." Gender differences related to empathy are not as black or white as it is often reported in the business literature to be. More importantly, thanks to neuroplasticity, empathy can be cultivated. It is not fixed at birth and both genders have access to it.

I do wish to note that, as the author of the Barrett research pointed out, the role of social conditioning is very real. In fact, early on in the report, Hannah Lee refers to research conducted by Marie-Helene Budworth and Sara L. Mann entitled, "Becoming a Leader: The Challenge of Modesty for Women:"

> *According to social role theory, behavioral gender differences are caused by socialization where at a young age, males are encouraged and rewarded for being outgoing, and achievement oriented. Conversely, females are taught to be emotionally oriented and reserved in their interactions with others.*

I agree with the social conditioning issue, but based on my experience and current scientific research, I disagree with conclusions inferring that gender behavioral differences are biologically based. Also, as you will learn in the section below on Neuroimaging and Behavior, our thinking changes our brain and our brain changes our thinking. Research has revealed that how we think changes the brain and this is a dynamic, ongoing process that has been noted to be reversible in cases such as obsessive-compulsive thinking, for example.

Social conditioning can influence which side of the brain is chosen the most and under what circumstances. There are female leaders who, when they attempt to adopt the style of the dominant left-brain leader—aggressive, individualistic, and goal rather than people oriented—generally receive push back from both men and women. It is not a situation where "gender or biology made me do it" as much as it is the need to be socially accepted. This is a Level 2 Mammalian Brain explanation for need to belong. Now we can learn to harness this personality "changeability" to align with our authentic values. **We can learn to choose according to the need of the leadership moment if we are self-aware enough to skillfully involve our Level 3 neo-cortex brain flexibility.**

Not all leaders are a fit for all cultures. It is wise to understand where you best align in an organization's culture. Of course, many organizations need to change their culture if they want to survive. The overriding paradigm that occupies much of our corporate culture does not focus on the development of human capital as a means to improving profits. The world is a very different place than it was only a few short decades ago. The drive is on, however, toward including self-actualization as a necessary part of the work paradigm. The zeitgeist of our times is encouraging this shift.

"BATTLES" INCREASE STRESS AND REDUCE CREATIVITY

In addition to gender bias pushback, the Battle of the Sexes, as reflected by the metaphor of the battle between brain hemispheres, has other consequences as well. It causes us to work and live at the Level 1 Reptilian

Brain and the Level 2 Mammalian Brain, which are not particularly self-aware or helpful in many leadership situations.

Stephen W. Porges, PhD, is a professor of psychiatry and the director of the Brain-Body Center at the University of Illinois at Chicago. In 1994, Porges proposed the Polyvagal Theory that links the evolution of the vertebrate autonomic nervous system to the emergence of social behavior. The Polyvagal Theory provides a theoretical perspective from which to study and treat stress and trauma. When men and women feel threatened by each other, stress and tension are created. Given this contest, I would offer a useful acronym for **FEAR: F**ictitious **E**vidence **A**ffecting **R**eality. What we believe affects our perceived "reality." In order to evolve our leadership skill sets so that they are more emotionally intelligent, we need to get a handle on our perception of fear, competition, and stress.

Porges' research suggests that we can retrain our nervous system to turn off our evolutionary programmed defense systems. I can say with certainty from my own experience that this is possible. Not only have I done it, but I also have had clients to report that they too have experienced less stress and fear as they become more self-aware. There is also a tendency for phobias to fall away. We are not merely reactive robots unless we wire our brains—even if unwittingly—to behave in such ways.

What I have learned from experience about this "evolutionarily programmed defense system" is that it truly is programmable. Our society also reinforces a focus on fear generation—generation, after generation, after generation. It is time now to stop because the stress and worry are killing us. In my own past, I experienced phobias and fears, acted defensively 24/7, and struggled with expecting worst-case scenarios. My inner critic only contributed to the distress. I learned through a spiritual practice of quieting my mind and recognizing that *I* was feeding my "Reptilian Brain," that I could actually stop feeding it! Instead of continuing to accept that "my brain is making me do it," I stopped focusing on negativity and paid attention to where I placed my intention and focus. I developed mindfulness and took back my mind from the grip of worry and fear. I developed my sense of self-worth and confidence based on my right to exist as a human/spirit being, rather than based on fluctuating social labels or what I was "doing."

Fear limits our cognitive ability. If your life is threatened, you have good reason to fear, and your body's survival instinct can serve you well. Most of the fear we encounter on a daily basis, however, is psychological; it is a form of fiction, as in, "our version of the story." Too often, we create our fearful reality and we then blame it on the Level 1 "Reptilian Brain" because we haven't known how to reprogram our conditioned, competitive paradigm.

When in fear, it is difficult to think clearly. It hampers our verbal skills and makes us relationally inhibited. The relational aspects of the prefrontal neo-cortex of our brain go offline, and we constrict on all levels of our being—the spiritual, the emotional, the mental, and the physical. *As an aside, our "higher" prefrontal cortex is also involved in emotional regulation.* Historically, science relegated emotion only to the "Primitive Brain" (The Reptilian Brain is often referred to as "primitive") because of our tendency to subjugate emotion to thinking. The belief that emotion is only limited to the less highly evolved levels of our brain is simply **not true.**

When we feel threat or worry, our body prepares to run or fight, though there is also the possibility of "freezing." Also, others can intuitively sense our defensiveness and constriction and often interpret it negatively through their own judgment filters. The inability to manage fear is counterproductive to leadership because it impedes developing charisma and trust. People tend to actively avoid being open or vulnerable around those who are too intense or defensive.

Dr. Porges' research goals were to help people become aware of how to change their proclivity toward fear and withdrawal and, with present moment awareness, choose their responses within the context of the situation. This can relax the nervous system and keep our bodies and minds healthier and paradoxically safer. Hyper-vigilance and competitiveness can cause us to actually miss dangerous situations. Not only does fear constrict the physical visual field in our eyes, it can also cause us to make poor decisions as leaders. Fear therefore inhibits social engagement, a serious leadership dilemma. From my perspective, this is one of the objectives of simply understanding how to optimally operate your amazing brain.

NEUROIMAGING AND BEHAVIOR

I will now address the second factor in assessing how this science of the brain plays out in our everyday life, and that is: **The role of intention (feeling) and attention (focus) in creating experience and performance.** Also, it is very noteworthy how our behaviors can actually change our neuroimaging study results.

The Hannah Lee (2010) research conducted by the Barrett Values Centre only reported findings generated from participants in a 360-degree assessment. These findings are not incorrect, but they are perhaps incomplete because self-reported and subjective findings cannot be assigned to objective *biological* gender predispositions, as they often are. Self-reporting assessments are a good baseline for how one presently sees and responds to the world. Recent objective brain research, however, ***does not*** support the belief that cognitive behavioral differences are *biologically* based. I agree that socialization is at the root of these differences, but no substantiating *biological* evidence exists. You are invited to refer to prior references should you want to further your own analysis regarding the science of my conclusions. Beyond the science, however, I can state that my personal experience also aligns with the new research. If behavior is biologically hardwired, as in the case of eye color, I would not be able to change my behavior at will.

This brings me to yet another danger that I arrive at when reading articles about gendered differences. It is believed that simply because one finds differences in brain fMRIs between men and women, there exists a "hardwiring" based on gender—as if there is a biological basis for the finding and that men and women are born that way. This is simply of misguided inductive reasoning. In light of the neuroscience research showing that the brain changes itself with thought, feeling, and experience, deeper deductive reasoning might allow that when we change our focus and behavior, our brain activity rewires; therefore, the fMRI changes are transient. Referring to "Biology" when discussing gender cognitive differences implies "unchangeable," as does "hardwired," in the minds of most people given the outdated biology theories we were taught in school. It is not biological; it is mindset.

Keep in mind that the brain is so neuroplastic that it can rewire its own genome. Once we create a pattern of behavior in our physiology, the associated neurophysiologic brain response will actually show up on imaging. The brain, on a micro-anatomical level, is always changing. It has already been demonstrated, for example, that in OCD (obsessive-compulsive disorder), when thinking and thinking alone is altered, the "worry-circuit" in the brain will decrease in activity. ***The actual brain scan activity will change.*** fMRI studies of this nature are more like a snapshot in time rather than a permanent, genetic finding. When OCD patients changed their intention so as not to worry (recall that intention has a feeling aspect to it), and focused their thoughts and awareness on the fact that these were just "worry circuits," their brains changed in response. This simple example illustrates how we can retrain our brains by holding a clear intention and a focused attention.

Dr. Norman Doidge, a neuroscientist, also has said: *"Don't believe everything you think!"* The recognition of neuroplasticity is so powerful, it is being used to treat PTSD (Post Traumatic Stress Disorder) and schizophrenia with remarkable results. The average person's obsessive negative thinking and inner critic that can operate to hinder self-confidence and performance is not nearly as complicated as these diseases of the mind. I actually did for myself, at least ten years ago, some of the very things researchers are using in their studies now!

Just because you see a pattern response in the brain today does not mean it was "hardwired" from birth. Thought and experiences can change the architecture and physiologic responses of the brain. If a woman and a man have behaved in prescribed ways for decades, it's not surprising that there would be a difference noted on brain imaging. However, this alone cannot validate "hardwiring" because behavior, thinking and feeling can modify the anatomy and function of the brain. Researchers are finding more and more that nurture can trump nature.

WE CO-CREATE OUR REALITY

It may take some extra effort initially to learn how to retrain your brain. But if you have no time at present to take the first steps, why do you think the opportunity to undo the drama created by negative thinking and behavior will present itself later? This is the same trouble that sometimes manifests itself in large organizations. The leaders who do not make time to develop their "people skills" and engage employees in the beginning of projects will waste time, energy, and money when they need to begin again—or when long delays occur due to poor productivity. Happiness is not something to pursue; we can create it within ourselves by taking our brains back from the external voices that seek to distract us and steer our attention toward *their* agendas.

Your so-called "reality" is what you make of it. Reality is not objective; it is subjective. This is the power that intention and attention has to create our experience. Until now, we have not understood the power of clear intention and how to consciously choose to direct our attention. It is for this reason that self-awareness is very important. You need to understand **how** to best operate your inner technology, your mind and imagination, in order to begin the intentional process of changing by conscious choice.

This is likewise true for the epidemic of stress that we see in the world today. Stress is a killer and is responsible for 90–95% of disease. It is disease—because we are not "at ease." If you feel "overwhelmed," you are stressed. Stress is heavily psychological because it concerns **how** you see things and **how** you feel. You need to learn to retrain your "how," i.e., your perception. Of course, when you don't get enough sleep, exercise, recreation, or good nutrition you exacerbate your symptoms. When you are constantly over-extended and busy, and do not take the mental breaks needed for renewal, you will increase your stress. The power to break the cycle of stress that can severely hinder your cognitive and behavioral performance as a leader is in your hands. You must learn to retrain your brain and bring motivation to the table to do so. We must slow down to become more effective. We cannot continue to exhibit maladaptive, over-active (left-brain) behavior and expect inspiring results.

Stanford researcher and psychologist Carol Dweck's studies on mindset demonstrate that whether or not people believe their intelligence and behavior are changeable directly affects their achievement. Her studies show that there are people with a "fixed mindset," and they are more likely to make choices that keep them stuck where they are. They cling to their current belief systems and make very little space for open mindedness. Their intention is focused on being "right." When compared to groups of people that have a "growth mindset" where all other opportunities are equal, the fixed mindset people exhibit lower performance on tested skills, as well as a significantly less likelihood of being able to adapt and grow when challenged. Even the expectation of math performance, something I referred to previously, has been shown to be linked to the self-fulfilling prophetic nature of the fixed or growth mindset.

More often than not, you experience what you really believe. However, just as neuroplasticity allows us to form new beliefs and habit patterns, it is this same principle that can keep us stuck. If we lock down on thoughts that say, "I can't change," we are still applying neuroplasticity to that belief. We will focus on experiences that prove this belief so that we can be "correct," and we ignore evidence to the contrary. Our brains are designed to keep us "right." Within neuroscience, there are these adages:

"Nerves that fire together wire together" and "Neurons out of sync fail to link"

When you focus and create belief, you are literally creating neuro-nets or neuro-circuits in the brain that "wire together" and reinforce the brain connection. When you intentionally break the focus on a belief, and refocus your mind elsewhere, you break the old circuit connections. They weaken and lose their energetic charge. Consider the act of memorizing how to play on the piano a musical selection "by heart" (remember, heart is the subconscious as well) and then stepping away from the piece for six months. Chances are, when you next return to it, you will make more mistakes until you re-practice the selection because your neuro-nets weakened when you stopped playing. You stopped using them, so the brainpower went elsewhere.

This same concept relates to negative thinking. As a culture, we have been often so focused on lack, competition, and pessimism, that we have unwittingly reinforced these types of beliefs and enhanced the strength of the corresponding neuro-nets in our minds. The "Battle of the Sexes," and for that matter, the battles of life, first begin within ourselves, within our minds. We can reverse this habitual pattern (which can be a type of mild OCD in some people) and intentionally reinforce our happiness and empathy circuits through self-awareness. Once again, we can create "self-fulfilling prophecy" by reinforcing what we think with our intention (feeling) and attention (focus). When we feel good and are not in worry or fear, we have more energy, clarity, and a higher level of cognition.

If you think you can do a thing or
you think you can't do a thing—you are right.

— Henry Ford

This now aligns, in general, with recent research in neuroscience. Pessimists are people who tend to see things through a lens of pessimism, but optimists have a brain bias that is toward optimism. Reality is not objective in these types of situations in particular. Your reality is real—to you. The choice of happiness or stress and overwhelm is within our control, to a great degree. Whether it was learned or genetic, you can change it. We have not understood that it was possible to change, and we now are just learning how to consciously effect that change with greater ease and less effort.

There are two related lessons to this. One is that our inflexible attitude regarding the Battle of the Sexes is a result of our brain bias. The second is that the old paradigm that adults cannot change has a powerful influence on corporate policy regarding adult development and learning. Now that we are beginning to understand the misconceptions around both of these issues, we are better equipped to rethink our fundamental assumptions.

We can individually and then collectively begin to create a new paradigm. We can create a paradigm that allows for a level of business and leadership development that is more humane and does not greedily hoard or repress the potential in other human beings. Intention matters; how we view our "self" and others matter. And how the leader sees others can impact that leader's influence as well. People can feel judgment and sometimes, if they are not confident, the leader's belittling attitude can sabotage a team member's performance.

The role of self-identity is a major factor in how we see our world and our potential for leadership development. Let us now turn to the discussion of a related idea. *"Who do you think you are?"* is the subject of the next chapter. The practical "how-to apply" steps for the information I am sharing in this book will be provided in the last chapter. When learning a whole new way of thinking, you need to lay the foundation for terminology and have a basic understanding in order to be in command of your power of conscious choice. If only "how-to" skill sets were required to become an outstanding performer, we would all be over-the-top superstars by now. What has been holding us back is not a lack of information; it is a lack of emphasis and focus on understanding ourselves. Understanding **how** we create the story of our identity is critical to updating our "scripts" so that we can be adaptable, effective, and confident leaders in our constantly changing environments.

Key Points

- Our brain will find the things that it considers relevant to prove that we are "right," and virtually ignore the evidence that contradicts our current worldviews.

- Our brains are neuroplastic, and we are able to exercise and develop the strength of both our left and right brains with intention and practice.

- Think of the left-brain as "Head/Active" and the right-brain as "Heart/Receptive."

- We are most effective when we can access left-brain attributes (verbal, linear, analytical, structure, process, individualistic, active) and right-brain attributes (listening, imagination, intuition, context, metaphor, big-picture, relationship to others, receptive) as needed.

111

- Studies show that empathy is self-reported as low in men; yet, objective research findings contradict this—belief becomes our subjective experience.

- **FEAR** is typically due to *F*ictitious *E*vidence *A*ffecting *R*eality.

- The Battle of the Sexes contributes to stress and reduces productivity, leadership influence, and ultimately, innovation; in this regard, neuroplasticity is our solution.

- We can literally rewire our brains, and these changes are demonstrable via fMRI studies.

- Research indicates that we can consciously engage neuro-circuits that promote social engagement and increase our happiness.

- Happy employees are engaged, healthier, and more productive, thus increasing the likelihood of desired results that add to the "bottom line" of a company.

- We co-create our reality; the good news is we can choose to learn how to do this more easily.

Reflect: Inquiring Mind

1. What have you been in denial about: gaps in leadership development? Cultivating a clear and compelling vision?

2. How do you "justify" your status quo? What steps can you begin to take to proactively engage change?

3. How have you tended to lean too far to the left or right of your brain? Why does it matter to you to be able to access your "Whole Brain"? How could doing this help you in your career or business?

4. Do you tend to focus on what is missing or wrong, or ignore the good you have contributed? Have you thought about where you want to go or how your desired changes would look if they manifested?

5. Do you know what you really want? What brings you happiness?

Envision Possibilities

1. Instead of focusing on feelings of "overwhelm, stress, and what is 'wrong,'" envision the opposite of these current circumstances.

2. Feel **now** what you desire to have and you will begin to prime the pump for your brain and mind to seek it out and find the solutions for you. Repetition and expectation accelerate the process, making it "real" to your mind.

3. See in your mind's eye; hear and feel yourself being "creative" as you also imagine others acknowledging your innovative ability. Remember:

> *Imagination is the preview to life's coming attractions.*
> — Albert Einstein

CHAPTER FIVE

THE PRINCIPLE OF SELF-IDENTITY— "WHO DO YOU THINK YOU ARE?"

Thinking bravely is about achieving personal clarity.
It means knowing yourself so you can effectively lead others.

— Dean Sally Blount, '92 Kellogg School of Management,
Northwestern University

WHY IDENTITY MATTERS SO MUCH

Indeed, we are living in a time that requires innovation and sometimes even a whole new way of operating within the world. Leaders must be equipped to navigate change with great interpersonal skill. In order to keep pace with this rapid change, we may even be required to reinvent our very "self" and upgrade how we look at the world around us, including those we are called to lead. ***Our sense of self-identity is the driver of our choices, and it will determine what you think you can do, be, or have.*** Self-identity is the filter through which you perceive and act in the world. So, let me ask you,

"Who do you think you are?"

115

The answer can make or break your leadership effectiveness. People change and grow just as the environment continues to shift over time. Remaining "stuck" on the belief that how we show up in the world is "just the way I am" based upon current behavior leads to inflexibility and an inability to adapt. When we think of personal growth and development as something to avoid, it is little wonder we don't know ourselves. Not only have we tended to avoid discussions on gender, but we also avoid asking ourselves provocative questions. The gender arguments are only a symptom of a greater dilemma, which is the tendency to avoid what makes us uncomfortable.

Shutting down discussion is self-defeating and impedes progress.
— Sheryl Sandberg, author of *Lean In*

In the previous chapter, I have presented the evidence that we can change. Central to this chapter is our need to address the question:

Can women and men unlearn conditioned behaviors that limit leadership skill and constrict their vision of their personal and professional potential?

Our leadership and performance challenges go beyond gender. Perceived so-called limitations such as gender, low confidence, and fear of change can all be proactively improved or adjusted when one can consciously access the leadership advantage of brain awareness. Our brains are naturally wired to adapt and change our self-images and our performances if we are willing to learn and grow our "selves."

I find it fascinating how the brain can be so programmable when it comes to self-image (literally this is a brain "image"), self-talk, and behavior. Gender myths affect "who we think we are" and hence, impact our behavior. Besides gender, there are a host of other self-doubt creating beliefs, such as:

- I didn't go to the "right" school.

- I grew up on the "wrong" side of town.

- I don't have the money or connections.

- I'm too old to learn new skills.

- I'll embarrass myself if I make a mistake.

- I'm supposed to know it all.

- If I don't act tough, they won't listen to me.

- I feel like a fake.

- I'm not good enough or something is "wrong" with me.

- I'm afraid I can't do it. What if I fail?

This list could go on and on. We have not realized that we have the power to turn down the volume and even turn off these self-defeating voices in our heads.

This concept also is critical. If you believe that "men are this way and women are that way," not only do you limit your own true potential, but you also prejudice your mind when you encounter other people. If you are low on confidence and don't even attempt to achieve a goal or new position, you will create a self-fulfilling prophecy—you won't receive what you desire! You will automatically lose objectivity because your brain has been prewired with a script, and this automatic script can only hinder you as a leader.

Just as glaucoma patients lose their vision because they are unaware of enlarging blind spots, leaders and the companies they lead can lose vision and miss opportunities that are vital to continued success because mindset blinds them. The very person with the brilliance to help you take your company to the next level could be eliminated just because you looked at him or her and made a negative assumption due to *your* own blind spot. Unwittingly, some blind spots are developed based on past experiences that may be related to old behaviors which at one time protected or served us in some way. Our own inner insecurities are often a particularly insidious source of these blind spots. We can continue to filter the world through these self-protective viewpoints, which are now sabotaging us, or we can take back the Steering Wheels of our minds. Recall that we assign meaning based on how we see the world *via* how we see ourselves. If our performance and outcomes are not what we'd like, the way to sustainable change is to get to the root of what drives our perception—our own personal "*story*"!

NAVIGATING THE FUTURE WITH EYES WIDE OPEN

Ignoring the scientific evidence that biology does not predetermine (hardwire) cognitive development is to ignore the reality of neuroplasticity. This is yet another potential blind spot. Just as we create the narrative of our lives using our brain's "autobiographical memory" capacity, we can change the story lines. The better use of human potential is to focus on solving our current performance and business challenges, not repeating mistakes from the past.

One important solution to our leadership dilemma regarding the need to improve performance is to get to know ourselves via our values, purpose, and how we can best train our brains to experience greater fulfillment and confidence at the office and at home. An enthusiastic employee is also more likely to be a productive one. When we come to know ourselves in this way, we can then also become more self-aware so we can engage better cooperation between men and women, among team members, and among department silos. We must first be willing to see ourselves as evolving, learning and growing in order to proactively engage at this level. Simply chasing after new skill tactics without fundamentally understanding how we are unwittingly inhibiting our own performance is a waste of resources and time. We need to rise to the occasion and create a paradigm that moves us forward as individuals as well as moves the company forward, setting the intention to support the good of the whole. Science is showing us the brain's remarkable capacity to adapt; now it is up to us as individuals to decide to grow and evolve, or stunt our evolution by clinging to the past.

If we are to realize our true potential as leaders, we must separate our sense of identity not only from stereotypes, but also from our own self-created limitations, even when these are created unwittingly. If a man must align his character with the "way men are," he cannot come from his authentic core because every man is not identical—no two people are. This characterizes women as well. Also, if we have over-identified with our limited current thoughts and self-image, this can play havoc with our confidence. Our self-images can grow and expand as our mindsets change.

I once had a client who believed that if he showed sensitivity toward his leadership team, he would be considered "weak." His leadership style was often overly self-controlled and data driven, without having explored the context or engaging a big-picture team vision. He kept his distance from employees and had developed a reputation for resistance to front-line suggestion. He believed that if he shifted his original plan, the course correction would give the impression that he was indecisive. Needless to say, his poor listening skill was viewed as arrogance and a disregard for the contribution of those around him. This only reduced productivity and, ultimately, the things he feared the most resulted—missed deadlines, employee turnover, and CYA (cover your ass) behavior. As it turned out, my client was raised in the military culture and experienced a rigid, "traditional" home life with a demanding, controlling father at the helm. Even though he thought he would never emulate his dad when he grew up, he could not shake the voice in his head that often reminded him to, "act like a man" (his father's version that is). He was curious about the idea of, "retraining his brain." During our coaching sessions, as he became more open to recognizing that his perception of "how a leader should be" was literally prewired and could in fact be rewired with specific tools and strategies, he began to integrate the mental exercises that I provided into his daily lifestyle routines. It was remarkable how quickly he was able to shift his style to a more open-minded approach. He often reported with surprise that he could "catch himself" before automatically responding. Instead of being constantly on guard and defensive, he began to consciously listen more attentively and address his team with a sense of curiosity rather than his typical authoritarian approach. This allowed for trust to develop, and his fear of conflict relaxed. Ultimately, the trickle-down effect from his leadership efforts improved team coherence and performance, which is no surprise. With his own change in perception regarding the importance of personal development, he became more aware of the need to provide opportunity for growth and development for other leaders and their teams as well.

As goes the leader, so goes the team.

Another client was facing an identity crisis when his corporation downsized and he was let go after over 30 years of service. He literally was struggling with the question, "Who am I now?" This question and having extra time on his hands surfaced thoughts and feelings that he didn't even realize were lurking under the surface. Even though he was looking for a job, he was discouraged because he felt shame and embarrassment when he encountered people he knew and they asked him how he was doing. By the time he engaged me, he had developed an "Inner Critic" that was keeping him up at night, which only exacerbated his feelings of stress. He specifically was looking for a way to, in his own words, "retrain his brain to shut up." After learning not only how to redefine his identity and reframe his belief that "Who I am is what I do," he was able to quiet the inner dialogue and recognize that a part of what was making his job search so challenging was that he had no clarity about what he wanted to do in the first place!

Due to his lack of vision, the mental chatter, and the (mistaken) loss of identity, he had been spinning his wheels in more ways than one. By becoming aware of how he was sabotaging himself from the standpoint of his brain, he was able to direct his attention and performance differently, as well as much faster than would have been possible without a conscious awareness of how to more purposefully operate his brain.

If you are **not** what you think—this constantly changes—and you are **not** what you do, then who are you?

THE PLACE TO BEGIN

We must examine our behavior compassionately if we wish to change it with greater ease. Changing behavior does **not** mean that something is wrong with you now. Your behavior is not, strictly speaking, your "identity." In other words, what you **do** behaviorally is not equivalent to *who you are*. To clarify who you believe yourself "to be" requires separating your identity from your roles, titles, and experiences. While your character (how you think, feel, and act) will be revealed by what you do, your character can change as well. How? By changing how you think, feel, and act! As one gains wisdom, one can change. The simplest way of defining true, core self-identity, is to reflect on your "essence." The essence of you is the stable, intangible *spirit self that moves into the activity of the physical,* and not the definition of yourself created by the physical dimension. The physical dimension is constantly changing. Compare this with the "autobiographical memory" that forms the ego. It is the brain-based story about who we think we are." The ego, meaning "I" in Latin, is constantly evolving with time, whether we are aware of it or not. The ego tends to associate what we **do or have** with who we are because it is derived from our conscious self-definition, which has been trained to be overly focused on the external.

121

Essence is the intrinsic sense of self, the life force, the spirit self from which consciousness flows. It is the source of authenticity that defines desired physical expression. Very few people have taken the time to reflect on this inner "heart" of their "self." It is the "real you,"—also termed "The Mindful Me," the "True Self," or the "Authentic Self"—the spirit and heart of you versus the "Ego/Mental Me" of your autobiographical memory that is formed by your brain through your experiences. If you want to have a stable, centered state of self-confidence, you will need to fundamentally have self-acceptance *now* and as you grow through the stages of your life. You will need to learn how to separate your sense of identity from successes and mistakes, from other people's opinions, and from your material possessions. All of these things constantly fluctuate.

Self-acceptance refers to the realization that the various "parts of yourself" or states of being in which you find yourself are changeable. It is essentially self-compassion. Self-compassion is so important that it is being studied in neuroscience as a topic unto itself. To have compassion doesn't mean you condone your behavior. It just gives you the space to observe yourself without judging yourself as bad or good. Self-compassion allows you to choose more freely instead of running away from looking at yourself objectively. It short-circuits feelings of shame. We grow and evolve more easily when we exhibit self-compassion instead of judgment. **You can express this "Authentic Self" through a myriad of activities and feelings/states of being; the challenge is not to define yourself by the activity or experience itself.** This is not an overnight process, but realization must begin somewhere. Now would be a good time to begin.

As soon as you trust yourself, you will know how to live.

— Goethe

"Yourself," as used above, means your inner Authentic Self. This is the source of self-awareness that can then consciously choose which "parts" of your ego personality are most aligned with how you can most effectively show up on the Stage of Life. This likely all sounds foreign because we typically spend very little to no time in self-reflection or "getting to know ourselves." We have no real "intrapersonal" relationship (inward focused personal relationship). This is an opportunity for real innovation in real life!

How does this distinction play out? You may notice that you carry the "energy" (the essence) of courage and kindness into a difficult board of directors meeting; even if on the surface you are nervous (an experience), at your core Authentic Self, you still have a sense of courage and kindness. It is from the core of you; it is from your heart. Just because you feel nervous in the moment does not mean you are a "nervous person" as a human being. You bring courage and kindness to the things that you do and will be seen by others as courageous and kind as a characterization (your character). If you acted contrary to this essence, you would feel incongruent. Our awareness of our inner self evolves over time as well. We typically think that "we are" our current thoughts and feelings instead of thinking of these as simply passing moments or perceptions. The stages of true self-discovery unfold; self-discovery is not a single act.

Interestingly, on the flip side, if you are very disconnected from your essence, you will tend to live in your head and judge yourself by the current self-image formed by your ego self-image. If your ego tends to feel insecure and you act confident on the surface, your inner critic is likely to remind you that you are a "fake." *When we believe we are the feelings and thoughts of our ego, we tangle up our identity into the experience.* When you know who you are, you can feel nervous without believing you are a nervous person at your level of being. It is simply a feeling devoid of judgment regarding your sense of value as a human being. These are two different things. However, you will need to "know" this at a heart-felt belief level, not just intellectually. With practice and focus, you can rewire your nervous system to reconnect with the more confident, not-afraid-to-be-vulnerable, real you. I used to struggle terribly with this. It was not until I learned how to rewire the tapes that kept my ego feeling insecure that the inner critic stopped the chatter. Our human ego is meant to be the vehicle for the individual self-expression of our greater essence and purpose. It is not a villain; it is a part of our nervous system wiring—literally. Also, investing time in self-reflection, which enabled me to reconnect with my essence, redefined for me "who I am." What a relief it has been!

CORE VALUES

Your core values are expressed from this "heart" of your being, i.e., your "core," as well. Sometimes your ego can get tangled into your values. While what you do in the world will change over time, if you are making time to reflect and be aware of this inner core self, you will sense it to be your stable center. It is a place of stillness and strength that is "good enough just because." Getting in touch with your deeper values fuels your clarity, confidence, and peace of mind. They act as a compass, especially during the storms of life. Then, from this center, you can grow and learn your life lessons and make your impact on the world while living your unique purpose. Your healthy, transformed ego can assist you in manifesting your life purpose instead of getting in your way. This is why you need to understand the brain science of your ego. **Doing so will free you to embrace growth as a leader instead of constantly being on the defensive to protect an insecure ego's sense of worth and value as a person.** Identifying yourself by your role and behavior keeps you on the track of self-protection and defensiveness. Because of this, most people are afraid of making mistakes; they see mistakes as a defect in their identity instead of just being a way to learn from one's behavior.

Many people have always thought of themselves as their outer, physical body and what they do or have, (a matter that may require some contemplation). There is much more true potential at your core, and you must intentionally tap it in order to find this gold. Notice that if you do not go "inside" and never reflect, it is all too easy to hook your attention only to the external way that you show up in the world. The external world would then define your identity, which would be ever fluctuating. Your outer-world activity could easily conflict with your inner essence, leading to lack of fulfillment, disillusionment, and feeling inauthentic without understanding why. If we would reconnect with our inner heart self, our outer expression in the world would be more gifted and powerful. We are then much more likely to experience clarity, purpose, and passion in the things that we do.

Hopefully you are able to see that what you presently judge about yourself is not really "who you are." Keep in mind the Obsessive Compulsive Disorder (OCD) behavior presented in the previous chapter. Activating our "worry circuits" can disempower us and cause us to identify with being a victim. This can paralyze us or, at the very least, make us less effective. Our inner essence becomes buried under self-images of defectiveness or unworthiness. As I have already cautioned, "Don't believe everything that you think."

No matter where you are as a leader, I invite you to suspend judgment about your current situation, or achievements and "failures" thus far. Everyone does the best they can with what they understand to be true at a given time in their lives. Some of our self-image was formed as a young child, when we didn't know that the adults around us were projecting their own beliefs onto us. Just because your second-grade teacher was insensitive, or perhaps your parent had a bad day and yelled at you, does not mean there was something wrong with you. However, children take everything personally (as do many adults). We are still holding these images within our cellular memory. I reemphasize the Carl Rogers statement from the preceding chapters:

The curious paradox is that when I accept
myself just as I am, then I can change.

— Carl Rogers

It is not within the scope of this book to delve deeply into the philosophy of human nature. However, my intention is to bring at least some awareness to the process of how we pick and choose "who we think we are." Since doing this is so unconscious, many people have adopted roles and neglected parts of themselves that keep them in a chronic state of insecurity and self-defensiveness. Life lived from this viewpoint can be a big threat to our well-being and happiness as well as a real hindrance to growing as a leader.

The habitual way that we choose our thoughts and feelings, and our subsequently formed ego personality self-identity, creates perceptions that influence motivation and reactions to change. Recall that ego is formed by "autobiographical memory." The story line evolves and changes with experience. For example, "I am a practicing doctor" eventually goes away with retirement (of course, you can maintain your title), and "I am a wife" stops after divorce. These are roles. If being a wife is who you are, then who are you after divorce? This is why some people "lose their identity." There are other story lines that say "I am smart"—until you compare yourself to someone smarter than yourself—or "I am stupid"—until you find your unique genius. The point is, these are all valid roles and experiences; but if a person attaches his or her identity to it, the identity is shaky at best.

HOW YOUR MAMMALIAN
LEVEL 2 BRAIN HIJACKS IDENTITY

When we don't engage our higher levels of brain awareness, such as our Prefrontal cortex of our Thrival Level 3 brain, we seek our sense of security, love, and self-esteem only from external elements. Our focus on fear and competition keeps us on the hamster wheel of seeking security, love, and self-esteem. This is a symptom of living in our Survival Brain on Levels 1 and 2. If we think we are our ego mental concepts, we won't have a stable center. It is our lack of self-knowledge that keeps us "looking for love in all the wrong places." This shows up as needing validation from others before (or if ever) giving it to ourselves, being a, "pleaser" to your own harm, and always feeling insecure about money. It is the basis for greed. If you have a disconnected sense of self-worth, your ego will tend to set up a paradigm that you are better than someone else as long as you have more money than they do. The problem is, "enough is never enough." Money can disappear overnight and then again the question "Who are you?" surfaces. It is through the metaphoric door of the Thrival Level 3 brain that we can access awareness of our deeper spirit.

Know Thyself.
— Inscription on the Temple of Apollo at Delphi

It has been our over-identification with defining ourselves based on the outer labels and judgments of the day and our lack of inner reflection on our core spirit self that are the causes of so much insecurity. We look for our love, security, and self-esteem outside of ourselves instead of pausing to reconnect with our inner spirit. This is the spirit of you that leaves your body behind at the end of your life on earth. When you learn how to derive your sense of love, security, and self-esteem from this "real you" that is connected to all of "Life," you will realize that you are worthy of life because you exist! You are not simply an isolated human being. You are here and that means you are not an accident. You are valuable because you are a living human being. You were created and possess unique talents for a purpose. It is important to begin here with this understanding; then, you can cultivate the seeds of "magnificence" that are your unique styles and ways of contributing. Your leadership skills and styles can be integrated from this vantage point. There are no two people that are totally identical for a reason. This is a fundamental key to creating sustainable performance as you become self-secure enough to be willing to embrace change with an open heart. How you tend the garden of your mind will determine whether or not you blossom as a leader. This is the path to getting off of the hamster wheel of self-judgment and comparing yourself to others. This is the path to "Be YOU, *Magnificently.*"

> *Be yourself; everyone else is taken.*
>
> — Oscar Wilde

The more we become aware of the influence that environment has had in molding us, the more mindfully we can approach our personal development.

I have had clients who have swung from one extreme to the other in their leadership styles before coming to the realization that neither extreme worked well for them. One female client of mine told me that she was attempting to be "more feminine" because she had been so controlling and domineering in the past. However, her attempt to work from consensus, which was her version of female leadership, was not working. In fact, she felt that her employees were overstepping their boundaries and losing respect for her. Since then she has realized that, from an "Authentic Self" perspective, she is strong with a gentle heart, and she has been able to engage more consciously in erasing old tapes about how she "should behave" as a woman, or how "people run over you if you are weak." The truth has been that, as she becomes more self-aware, she is able to speak her truth without stripping others of their space to be heard. Likewise, she feels more confident to just say "no" without guilt. She is on the path to discovering what feels most authentic for her and how to be a more situational leader. She is no longer simply acting "reactively" from old, outdated patterns of thinking and acting.

FEELINGS SHAPE EMOTIONAL INTELLIGENCE

Since feeling is the glue that deeply wires our cellular memory, you would be wise to acquaint yourself with your own. Feelings define our experience. As discussed previously, feelings play a powerful role in forming "belief," even as these relate to beliefs about our self-identity. When we are aware that there is a distinction between our feelings and "who we are," we can better self-manage them more mindfully. Self-managing our feelings, however, is tricky because most people fear their feelings as if they are "bad." As Shakespeare noted:

Nothing is good or bad except thinking makes it so.

Labeling feelings as "bad' is a judgment, and doing this is not in your best interests because how you perceive feelings determines how you experience them. They color your life and inform you about how you are reading a situation. This strongly influences our emotional intelligence. Emotional Intelligence (EI or EQ) is not simply about taking a certification course and learning some "new tricks." Daniel Goleman notes in his book, *Primal Leadership, that* your emotions are at the heart of effective leadership. In order to apply EQ, you will need to acquaint yourself with, of all things, your emotions!

How each of us sees our self-identity contributes to emotional intelligence as it relates to how we "feel" about ourselves. If we as leaders do not address our inner insecurities, they can spill over into how we relate to people and hinder application of our EQ skills. While I am a champion of the recent surge of interest in emotional intelligence, there is also an underpinning of emotional intelligence that is connected to the management of feelings that I have not seen specifically addressed. As I pointed out in chapter three, emotions and feelings are not synonymous, but both are involved in the formation of our perception. In fact, they are the basis of perception. They address the instantaneous subconscious question: Is the person, situation, or circumstance in "resonance" with you or in "dissonance" with you?

In other words, do you "like" or "dislike" who/what you are observing? Feelings are the bodily response you have to that perceptual interpretation. Even when armed with the knowledge and skills to recognize gaps in EQ within your behavior, without also learning how to change your perception about feelings and better managing them physiologically as well as intellectually, your new EQ skill sets can be hijacked by your bodily response to your feelings before you realize what hit you. We have been conditioned to feel shame about our feelings. Most people equate "vulnerability" with their experience of feelings—and interpret this as weakness. Actually, it takes courage to be vulnerable. It takes fearlessness—"less fear." Your discomfort within a given situation can activate your "survival instinct" and stress very quickly, which is also what makes people fear change. Hence the need for each of us to "know who he or she is" in order to hold a state of equanimity when coming into contact with a diversified work force. This is why self-awareness via skillfully accessing our Thrival Level 3 brain is so important. Our confidence is directly linked to our ability to self-manage our emotions.

What Makes Emotion So Scary?

There can be many reasons why emotions are scary to us, but for purposes of this discussion, I would suggest it is attributable to generational ignorance about our emotions. It is our perception(s) about emotions that make them so challenging. Children are very emotional. They do not have developed logic, but they certainly express their unadulterated feelings! Research is now demonstrating that early in life, our right-brain hemisphere—the more emotional brain, is dominant. Our identity is forming without much logic or understanding regarding the story we tell ourselves about ourselves.

As children, we adopted our behaviors for love and approval and created childish stories about who we thought we were in the world. I say childish because, based in the experience of a young child—who is not very sophisticated generally speaking, we adapted to external forces. Depending on our temperament, environment, and even birth order, we formed a sense of self-identity. Considering how fearful a child's imagination can be, especially when accompanied by the uncensored feedback from teachers and insensitive peers, childhood and the teen years can be traumatic to our self-confidence. These negative feelings are not well managed, and there often comes a point in time when children "grow up" and adapt to their environment by "shutting down" their emotional guidance system. This is a type of self-defense mechanism to protect the heart from feelings of insecurity in one's formed identity. The personality that we assume from these experiences is, more often than not, also based on self-protection and survival. This is how we form the ego "parts of our self"—our personality—in early childhood.

An entertaining movie that I enjoyed over a decade ago exemplifies quite well how this mentally constructed process occurs. The movie was titled, *The Kid,* and Bruce Willis starred as the main character. I was grateful for this movie at the time because it helped to show my husband what I was talking about in terms of what I was doing to change my own behavior! Briefly, this movie is about how we "get stuck" in early childhood, owing to the stories we create in our minds as a result of emotionally stressful situations. Bruce Willis' character, as a child, came to think of himself as defective or not good enough, and blamed himself for something he could not have prevented. Before he began to recognize its source, this self-created self-image drove him for many decades to aggressively over-achieve as a way of compensating for his insecure identity. This mental construct of himself created a personality that was not very likeable, and made him miserable as well. These "parts of our self" get formed in this fashion and unconsciously drive us. When we become aware of this process, we can address it objectively and "update" our self-image with greater maturity.

Few people are likely to escape the traumas of childhood with their authenticity intact. In fact, the "survival of the fittest" paradigm encourages comparison and competition with others. Feelings and emotions then become the "enemy," and the need to control is always at the forefront of the mind for many (especially men). Escaping to the left-logical, external-world focused brain to avoid feeling is an extremely common self-defense mechanism. Women are allowed more space for the heart—their feelings, compassion, and intuition—even to the point of labeling this as "a woman's intuition." I would suggest that this is another misnomer because I've met quite a few intuitive men in the business world as well. There are men who are tapping the qualities of their right-brain whether they realize it or not.

If we are going to be present to a situation and not be self-deceived by "intellectualized emotion" (denial), we will need to "make friends with our feelings." Thus, we must learn how to reframe the meaning of feelings so that our nervous system stops over-reacting to them. Paradoxically, when we change the way we perceive feelings, they tend to calm down. We can accelerate this process when we rationally engage our logical mind by learning what feelings are triggered by a situation and recognizing their power in the creative process. Happiness research and the science of feelings are now bringing this conversation to the forefront. And it is critical.

Feelings Are at the Heart of Leadership Skill

It was not until I stopped feeling terror at the thought of feeling vulnerable, or feeling my feelings, that I really began to grow and develop rapidly as a leader. I have clients who, on the surface at work, act like the stereotypical command-control boss, but in coaching, express their desire to show their more empathetic side. They are just "afraid" that they will not be perceived as strong, or that they will lose control. Likewise, I have other clients who want to assert themselves more, but when they do, they feel anxiety. Their subconscious subtle memories of being rejected by those around them for speaking up and voicing their opinions when they were younger, or even currently, are likely to account for these feelings. Thus, the "parts of our self" play out on the Stage of Life. Because people dread their feelings, they sometimes hold themselves back. These clients did not understand how to diffuse their automatic reaction to act compliant until they worked with me as their executive coach.

Self-management of feeling is tied to the health of teams and organizations. Team dysfunction and employee engagement require healthy communication. Without the ability to communicate explicitly, misunderstanding and lack of accountability abounds. Our incompetency with handling our feelings is at the root of poor handling of courageous conversations. It is one thing to talk about having these important conversations; it is another thing to "walk" it out. Our fear of our feelings is a source of our tendency to blame as well. Until we learn to more skillfully manage our feelings and our sense of identity, having healthy, courageous communication that builds trust is a mere pipe dream.

As clients use the tools that I share to help them better self-manage their feelings, they report that they not only have the desired results, but they also feel more relaxed and confident. Learning to separate your sense of self from your thoughts and noticing your feelings—"mindfulness"—has now garnered quite a bit of research that documents how one can have more emotional stability and better self-manage by developing these skills. For this reason, the practice of mindfulness is one way to improve emotional intelligence. It gives you space between the emotion-provoking experience and your reaction time so that you can actually apply your EI skills. I will say more about mindfulness meditation in chapter eight in the "Tips and Strategies" section. In order to set the stage for better understanding about why mindfulness is so vital to taking back the Steering

Wheel of your Mind, let's explore a bit more deeply the major roles of these parts of ourselves. In that process, we will realize that some parts play starring roles and some play bit parts. As we shine the spotlight on these inner characters of our mind, we are better able to bring them into the Light of Transformation so that they can further support our Authentic Self instead of keeping us stuck.

THE FEAR OF CHANGE

Our survival instinct will overrule our empathy towards others if we are on hyper-alert to protect ourselves from "the competition." If we see others as a threat and feel insecure in our positions, change will surely be our mind's enemy. The more we overemphasize our differences and create organizations that ignore trust and communication, the more difficult it will be for that organization to navigate change. When we have an undeveloped ability to manage our feelings and have a sense of self-identity that is shaky from childhood, we create a psychological environment where the "Inner Critic" can thrive. The inner critic inhibits our ability to adapt to change. You will not be able to get a grip on your inner critic until you learn how to accept yourself "as you are for now" and realize that you are constantly in the process of growing and evolving throughout your life. Your current version of yourself is only a snapshot in time. I've already emphasized that self-acceptance makes personal growth and development much easier. This understanding is just a part of the human journey.

Yet, as you understand your brain better, you will realize that you are ever able to grow. You will learn how to optimally manage your energy, exercise better self-care overall, and retrain your brain to be more effective. You can change your inner image to align with your natural strengths, and bring to light the weaknesses or gaps that need your attention if you are to develop into a whole, integrated human being and, subsequently, a better leader. You will access on purpose both sides of your brain instead of ignoring one side or the other. As you quiet the left-brain, you can better cultivate the awareness of your Authentic Self by connecting with your inner world through your right-brain and what is purposeful for you. Then, you can be "pulled" toward your vision with excitement and enthusiasm instead of being driven there by fear of failure. You can be authentically secure within yourself. As stated by Dean Sally Blount of Northwestern University in the opening quotation to this chapter, this will require "thinking bravely."

When we realize that we are suppressing authentic parts of our "self" to align with the expectations of gender roles, we can address our blind spots. Some command-control male leaders behave in this manner because they feel that it is expected of them in order to be perceived as a "strong leader." That may have been true at one time, but this type of behavior has now become a handicap. It is important, as illustrated from these examples, to recognize how self-image and autobiographical memory impact our leadership performance story line. This lack of understanding about how we can change who we think we are, and how our thoughts and feelings impact our performance, is a major reason why leaders are challenged when it comes to walking their talk or applying skill sets they have learned. We must develop our mindset as well as our skill set.

ENVIRONMENT AND CULTURE IMPACT BEHAVIOR

Your behavior is not a snapshot in time; you are ever-evolving. Your environment can powerfully influence your behavioral choices. If you are not mindful, you may unconsciously believe that your responses are "just the way you are"—your identity.

We know, for example, that company culture influences behavior. In environments that foster competition, rewards and "looking good" over substance, employee personality/behavioral profiles tend to differ from cultures that support explicit communication and accountability. The command-control leadership style is the norm in many cultures and, if one is not clear about his or her own values and "authentic" behavior, it is all too easy to slide into the mold that is culturally, tacitly expected. When I was in medical school, I adopted a strong command-control style. Later, while leading my medical practice, I came to grips with the fact that this style felt incongruent with my authentic core and, consequently, I made it a goal to change to a more collaborative style that was sustainable. And it worked!

Life experiences in total look more like a kaleidoscope of personalities and roles. The question is, are you taking on roles and behaviors that align with and feel like the "real you," or are you playing roles that were assigned to you by others? Also, when we hold cellular memories from earlier times in our lives, we get stuck. This stunts our growth and development. When you hear yourself saying, "This is just the way I am"—meaning that even though you really may want to change, you think you cannot—ask yourself whether you are simply stuck on those cellular memories.

Until we get in touch with our purpose and passion, it is challenging to know what is authentic behavior for us. Many people have one personality at the office and another at home, and then they wonder why they feel "like a fake." Once we make the time to reflect on who we are and how this expresses from the heart into the world, then we can run activity through our "purpose filter" before moving forward. We can integrate our lives as a whole person. After all, you take "you" with you, wherever you go.

PUTTING IT ALL TOGETHER

Could these social norms regarding how men and women "should" act be linked to the "the battle of the sexes"—the power struggle? I believe so. It makes sense now to expand the context for this battle of the sexes to the battle between our left and right brain hemispheres (as metaphor). It is important to note, from the words of McGilchrist, "the hemispheres need to cooperate." In order to optimize our brain and make it most effective, the hemispheres should collaborate, and not engage in a power struggle. This metaphor is one to keep in mind as we explore potential solutions for the "Battle of the Sexes" currently experienced within the arena of leadership development. Perhaps we, as men and women, should take note of the admonition to "cooperate and not engage in a power struggle" so that we can maximize our own potential and the potential of our organizations. Of course, organizations are composed of individuals, and leaders have the greatest influence to effect change.

Notice the brain chart in the previous chapter and how the left-brain, especially the left-brain dysfunctional quadrant, describes "Macho male" behavior. The right-brain dysfunctional quadrant is often the stereotyped caricature of women. Given that our culture historically has overtly conditioned "men to be men" and "women to be women," according to the norm of the day, it is certainly plausible that the way that we have trained our brains to lateralize to the left or right contributes to how we "show up" in the world based on gender expectation. Of course, this is all subconscious.

In summary, what I am suggesting here is that our brains are able to adapt to our perceptions and needs to survive. If the cultural influence is to reward left-brain behavior in men and the opposite in women, then the brain is likely to respond, "your wish is my command." Even when a woman chooses to consciously exert her will to change her behavior and adopts more of her left-brain characteristics into her behavior, she is still sometimes pressured to stop this process and retreat back into "acting like a woman." Then, when she reverts back to behaving passively and becomes the caretaker, she creates a "self-fulfilling prophecy." She starts to act like the stereotype of a woman, and her behavior gets ascribed to biology. This is another way of describing a self-fulfilling prophecy.

The understanding of how we create self-fulfilling prophecy is an important point to understand if you want to begin tapping into your "authentic" true potential. You are not a pre-programmed robot, but you must know how to change your inner technology if you want to stop acting like one. The 21st century leader will need to come from a sense of rooted and grounded identity before she or he can ever hope to be a situational leader. Being able to listen, maintain an open-mind, and respect the diverse life experience of others while inspiring cooperation and efficiency requires the utmost self-confidence and inner security. Tapping into neuroplasticity, the adaptability of our brains makes this a real possibility.

If you want to improve your leadership skill and capacity with greater rapidity, you will need to change your playbook and adopt some new rules for thinking and feeling. At the root of developing into an engaging effective leader is willingness to take responsibility—"response-ability"—for learning how to retrain your brain to a higher functioning level. As discussed previously in this chapter, *you may need to retrain how you see yourself as well.* Instead of seeing everyone as a threat to your well-being and safety, learn how to see yourself as empowered and able to rise to the occasion, with strength and compassion.

Okay, so now that you have seen what is possible in terms of your own leadership growth and the role that self-identity and feelings play in this process, where do we go from here? In part II of this book, you will learn how to begin applying what you have learned thus far, first by identifying your leadership style tendencies, and then by exploring how it might look theoretically (in terms of examples), if your brain hemispheres could work more collaboratively instead of struggling against each other. The final chapter of this book will contain practical exercises you can do to help you get unstuck and learn more effective behaviors. However, it is vital that you allow your left-brain to engage in these exercises by understanding beforehand what is going on logically. If you bypass working toward an understanding of the science, your logical mind may just talk you out of doing the exercises altogether. Remember, there really is a difference between knowing (about) the path and walking the path. Practical, contextual application is the path to situational, self-aware leadership that inspires loyalty and engages effective productivity.

Key Points

- Our sense of self-identity is the driver of our choices; it will determine what you think you can do, be, or have.

- Self-identity is the filter through which you perceive and act in the world.

- When we think of personal growth and development as something to avoid, it is little wonder why we don't know ourselves.

- Perceived so-called limitations, such as gender, low confidence, and fear of change can all be proactively improved or adjusted when one can consciously access the leadership advantage of brain awareness.

- We must realize that we have the power to turn down the volume and even turn off self-defeating voices in our heads.

- To ignore the scientific evidence indicating that biology does not predetermine (hardwire) cognitive development is to ignore the reality of neuroplasticity.

- If we are to realize our true potential as leaders, we must separate our sense of identity not only from stereotypes, but also from our own self-created limitations—even when created unwittingly.

- We must examine our behavior compassionately if we wish to change it with greater ease; it is a question of getting to know ourselves.

- Self-acceptance refers to the realization that the various "parts of yourself" or states of being in which you find yourself are changeable. This is essentially self-compassion.

- Your healthy, transformed ego can assist you with manifesting your life purpose instead of getting in your way. **You must therefore understand the brain science of your ego.**

- When we don't engage our higher levels of brain awareness, such as the Prefrontal cortex of our Thrival Level 3 brain, we seek our sense of security, love, and self-esteem only from external elements. This is a symptom of living in the Survival levels of our brain.

- The more we become aware of the influence that environment has had in molding us, the more mindfully we can approach our personal development.

- Feelings strongly influence our emotional intelligence. Thus, self-awareness via skillfully accessing our Thrival Level 3 brain is critical.

- Few people are likely to escape the traumas of childhood with their authenticity intact. In fact, the "survival of the fittest" paradigm encourages comparison and competition with others.

- Feelings are at the heart of leadership skill.

- Our survival instinct will overrule our empathy towards others if we are on "hyper-alert" to protect ourselves from "the competition."

- There likely exists a link between the attributes of the "battles" within our brain hemispheres and the historical "Battle of the Sexes." The divided brain has "theoretically" created a divided gender culture.

- Understanding how we create self-fulfilling prophecy is an important concept if we want to begin tapping into our "authentic" true potential.

- The more self-aware we become of the script that we write for ourselves, the more control we can have over accessing our own co-creative life experiences as human beings— *regardless of gender.*

Reflection: Inquiring Mind

1. Who do you think you are? Why do you think this?

2. How does the way that you currently see yourself differ from your "Ideal Self"? What are the characteristics of this Ideal Self?

3. How does the way that you see yourself influence your behavior around others?

4. How do you think your assumptions about how "people are" or how "the world is" create blind spots in your leadership performance? Is it holding you back in any way?

5. If you had self-mastery over feelings as they arise or change, how would you respond in situations of employee turnover? Low performance? Courageous conversations? Are you willing to explore changing your perception about feelings?

Envision Possibilities

1. Imagine in your mind's eye how you walk, talk, dress, feel, and think as your Ideal Self.

2. When you imagine living as your Ideal Self, what is the character and qualities of those with whom you surround yourself? What is the quality of your relationships with others?

3. How would you show up as a leader? What would this look like in "reality"? (Imagine your future "reality" now).

PART II: MINDING OUR BUSINESS WITH A MINDFUL BRAIN

Your job as a leader is to take people from where they are today to where they need to be tomorrow, do so as quickly as possible, and do it in a way that is sustainable.

— Doug Conant, former CEO of Campbell Soup Company
and author of *TouchPoints*

CHAPTER SIX

LEADERSHIP TENDENCIES— WHAT'S YOUR STYLE PREFERENCE?

In times of change, learners inherit the earth.

— Erich Fromm

WHERE ARE YOU NOW?

Our personal leadership tendencies ultimately form the culture of our companies and organizations. This is a dynamic that is often overlooked. Based on their own behavior, leaders create the structures and styles of leadership that give rise to the invisible power of "organizational structure," which is the container for supporting culture. Hence, there is a dance between self-assessment and how we perceive the external world, and creating the outward structures that lead to the formation of culture. In order to get where you want to go, you need to assess where you currently are personally and then organizationally. There is a simple analogy to using the GPS system in your car. Without knowing your starting point, reaching your destination will be challenging at best.

In a Harvard Business Review article from February 17, 2012, entitled **"A New Era for Global Leadership Development,"** Harvard

Business School Professor Bill George referenced the need for leadership style change in an example of cultural restructuring at IBM. Samuel Palmisano, IBM's former chairman and CEO is known for having reorganized the company into an "integrated global enterprise" in 2003. George points out that leading by values and collaboration empowered leaders to extend IBM's culture globally.

The structure of traditional, hierarchical leadership often supports the command-control style and is not inclusive. This leads "naturally" to silos and the fear of authentic communication. This style of leadership can omit vital information for the organization and provoke heart disengagement, leading to lack of loyalty from employees since, by definition, it is neither engaging nor collaborative.

In the previous chapter, I illustrated how our sense of "who we think we are" guides our behavior. In this chapter, you can administer a simple evaluation to give you an idea of how you currently see yourself behaviorally, and how your choices reflect either left-brain characteristics or right-brain characteristics. This Leadership Evaluation tool is not meant to be "scientific" and (of course) its outcome is self-reported. Bias is therefore a possibility. With that in mind, do your best to approach this exercise with an open and curious mindset. The point of this evaluation is to begin recognizing the ways in which we tend to habitually engage with the world and how we, in theory, tend to lateralize to one hemisphere style or another. The more conscious we become in using this concept as a model, the more self-aware we can be about shifting our behavior. We can then appreciate how "mindset" can lead to the structures that form our organization's culture—a culture that impacts employee levels of productivity and performance.

A less critical, but still important, point to note is that these self-reporting personality tests, while subjective, do tend to reveal what I might term "surface" personality behaviors. I say "surface" because I want you to be aware that there is a deeper "True Self." There is a strong tendency for people to believe that the profile that emerges from these tests is "who they are." Generally speaking, however, that is not the case. More often, this profile reflects, "who you think you are," which is how you are currently showing up in life. But this kind of profile evolves.

It is best to remember that these types of tests only reflect where you are at the moment—a snapshot in time. They reflect your current behavior or at least your own image of yourself. DiSC® is a commonly used behavioral assessment tool in the business world. My DiSC® profile has evolved over time as I have evolved, and the changes have been quite stark. As a leader, I once was very commanding—without any real balance. Now I'm equally Di with some of SC. (Please refer to your own references for more information on DiSC®.) What is noteworthy is that I am also "affirming" which, according to the test, is atypical for a person with a Di profile. The point is, we cannot be defined by a simple test. We have the ability to adapt and reconnect with lost parts of our "self "as we become more self-aware. My behavior is not "hardwired" and unchangeable.

In order to lead change in an enlightened way in the present moment, a leader must continuously learn how to expand his or her self-awareness in order to develop to the next level. There is no final destination point. We are all continuously growing and evolving. The more we embrace this virtually untapped ability, the easier it will be to fluidly adapt to our constantly changing environment in a way that is effective.

Leaders and their team members will need to grow personally and professionally in order to improve communication skills, emotional intelligence, and develop the willingness to keep learning and evolving new technical skill sets. The business world must evolve its leadership models in order to bring innovation to the style of "The Boss"— who is otherwise considered a command-control leader. As noted earlier in this work, that style has a tendency to disengage people, which means lowered performance and job satisfaction in the workplace. Even more problematic, it raises the probability that both the leader and the organization will become irrelevant. Leadership styles impact the organizational leadership structure and culture and, ultimately, performance and profits. A more adaptive leadership model is needed.

LEADERSHIP STRUCTURES AND STYLES

Is hierarchy leadership always "command-control"?

I often hear the words "hierarchy" and "command-control" used interchangeably. I would like to distinguish between these words within the context of this discussion. I view hierarchy as a type of container or structure, and command-control as a type of style within this structure. In the same way that we want to integrate and use the whole brain, the innovative company integrates both the traditional and collaborative structures. Let's look at three types of overall leadership structures.

Structures

The first and more traditional structure consists of a "hierarchy." It is based on levels or tiers of authority. It has a pyramidal shape, with increasing authority vested in each individual leader as one moves higher in the chain of command. This structure has a long history of use in the military, healthcare, education, politics, and the workplace—to name just a few examples. And it has been used ubiquitously in our society. Hierarchy allows for structure and order, particularly when decisions require ultimate authority; it is especially useful in the context of large social groups. The hierarchical structure provides a sense of safety and security because people have a degree of social predictability. Like all behavioral models, there are degrees of expression along a spectrum. Hierarchy does have some downsides, however, particularly when used by a leader with an inflexible mindset. For example, the rigidly hierarchical leader tends to make decisions in isolation because communication is not likely to be open within this type of culture. There tends to be an atmosphere of intimidation. Often, when people don't feel that they are heard or have an opportunity for development, passive-aggressive behavior in its varied manifestations is not uncommon. In this day of rapid market change and volatility, an organization marked by this structure is at a serious disadvantage.

The second structure is that of "collaborative leadership." I want to emphasize that this structure is not the same as "consensus." It is an innovation made to the traditional hierarchical model, but there is still a chain of ultimate responsibility and accountability. It is a model that metaphorically engages our left and right-brain hemispheres, as described earlier. It has the needed (left-brain) structure in place to provide accountability, process, and order, yet it allows for flexibility (right-brain) that gives space to employee/team member input, ownership, and alignment. It is the path to engaging the mind and heart of all stakeholders involved in a project. In short, it is visionary with structure and process.

Collaborative leadership also is a more expedient path than the hierarchical for eliminating team dysfunction due to poor accountability and commitment. Leaders cannot force heartfelt commitment and passion. The more the leader develops skills of self-awareness, empathy, insight, and the ability to empower people, the more loyalty, cooperation, and productivity he or she is likely to achieve. Collaborative leadership as a structure requires a higher level of individual emotional intelligence and self-mastery within a leader than does the rigid hierarchical leadership structure. While there may be differences of opinion, at least the procedures and processes are explicit, and organizational communication processes are evolved in a way that affords the space for stakeholders to be heard. Employees who feel that they are valued and heard are much more likely to give their best effort. Collaborative structures facilitate the mind and heart engagement of the team. Of course, at the end of the discussion, the leader is ultimately responsible for the outcome and still has the power to control the final decision.

The third type of leadership structure often discussed is consensus leadership. In this situation, the goal is to have all persons agree on a given decision. This is a challenging format for the work environment. In fact, it is challenging at times even with two or more people. It is nice in theory that all people align on all issues all the time, but that is likely to be a rare occurrence at best. Consensus is based on agreeable, healthy relationships and a sense of community. Yet individuals are on different levels of emotional intelligence and have differing agendas and perceptions about the meaning of situations. Given this reality, consensus is not likely to be effective or efficient. It is simply not pragmatic in the corporate workplace.

If you refer back to the Brain Hemisphere Behavior Chart in chapter four on page 98 you may notice a pattern of extremes that can be applied to the three traditional structures of hierarchy, collaboration, and consensus. In order to make the point more clearly, the "Dysfunctional" left-brain quadrant in a hierarchical structure allows for extremes in command-control behavior listed in this quadrant. Likewise, the right-brain quadrant "Dysfunctional" side would more likely be operative in a strictly consensus environment. *Collaborative styles incorporate a more integrated **"Functional"** dynamic of the two hemispheres—a collaboration of the brain hemispheres.* When a leader can integrate strategy and process with engagement of the heart of the people on the team, he or she is demonstrating collaboration between their own brain hemispheres. This is the ultimate goal—it's not a matter of either/or; it's both. As a self-aware leader, you can flow through a toolbox of leadership styles that all reflect your values and tap into the best of your human capabilities that support dynamic, inspiring leadership and culture (see the following section on styles). One need not rigidly cling to a certain type of leadership style. Self-awareness allows for mental agility.

Various Styles of Leadership and Their Integration into Structure

Beyond structure, there is one's leadership "style." A cogent discussion of leadership styles can be found in Daniel Goleman's book, *Primal Leadership*. In this book, Goleman identifies six leadership styles. He lists these as:

1. Visionary

2. Coaching

3. Affiliative

4. Democratic

5. Pacesetting

6. Commanding

Each style carries its own nuances that can be most effective in a given situation. The key to effectiveness is flexibility and range. Mental agility will make or break one's ability to access these various styles on demand. Leadership is not a one-size-fits-all proposition. A rigidly command-control style, whether you are male or female, is not likely to produce the most effective leader, particularly given the growing expectations for individual expression and contribution in our increasingly diverse workplace. Both hierarchical and collaborative structures can have more than one style or expression of leadership. Yet, unless collaboration is an ***explicitly*** expressed cultural structure, it is all too easy to default to the traditional hierarchical structure that supports command-control leadership style patterns.

For example, hierarchical and collaborative structures can have different styles of expression within them, but the overall structure is the container for the different types of styles. Both of these structures can integrate command and relational expression to varying degrees. Of course, it is quite apparent that "command-control" would ***not*** be a style routinely found within a collaborative structure though, at times, it may be required in an urgent situations. Command-control is as it sounds; it allows very little space for self-expression from others. In emergency situations, this can be necessary. Yet because it is so often inappropriately used, it typically has a negative impact on the organizational culture. Fear and intimidation are often involved, and the emphasis is on status and "power" over others. It cultivates and encourages the leader's focus on self-interest rather than a focus on the greater good for the organization in the long run. People are the heart and soul of an organization, and there is a growing need to develop leaders who have excellent "people skills" as well as tactile skill.

On the other hand, styles that foster cooperation between individuals and groups are more relational in nature and are likely to be the wave of the future—starting now. They are built on trust and a "power with others" model instead. They work best in collaborative leadership structures. As I mentioned previously, collaborative leadership is an innovation to hierarchical leadership. We don't throw out the old structure altogether; we simply need to update the model to adapt to our evolving environmental demands.

No More Business as Usual

The transition of cultures from hierarchy, with command-control styles, to a structure of collaboration with cooperative leadership styles is the challenge leaders currently face. Of course, it will require the male or female leader to examine their beliefs and behaviors. **This is at the heart of the innovation needed to move organizations into a higher level of functioning that lends itself to competitive advantage.** It's not just about scrambling for new product ideas or "quick fix" skills development. "Follow the leader" has never had more riding on the outcome, but now it must operate to create an organizational structure that can engage the hearts and minds of people to be effective. "As the leader goes, so goes the team" can be a positive adage when the leader steps up to inspire others through example. Leadership is about "people development," not bossing others around. Before we can change the world, *we will have to change ourselves.* And this requires courage.

As leaders become more confidently self-aware and resilient, they will be able to see beyond a narrow focus and broaden it to include the much-needed development of the people within the company. This leadership challenge includes personal development of both the leader and the team members as well. The old model of "managing people"—via "power over" people—is not to be confused with leading and inspiring the highest levels of performance *from* people. Ownership and heart engagement is the basis for dynamic leadership and sustainable performance—regardless of gender.

EVALUATE YOUR PRESENT STYLE

Given that we can adjust our behavior, pausing first to evaluate ourselves, is simply intended to give you a starting point for evaluating where you are on this right and left-brain spectrum. Again, I remind you that the brain hemispheres are ideally designed to support each other in integrative ways. There is not a black and white compartmentalization of function. Yet we must begin to help our intellect understand these rather "foreign" concepts that the new discoveries in neuroscience have revealed. So let us take a few minutes to respond to the following leadership evaluation statements.

After you have tallied your responses and identified your leadership style, proceed to the next chapter where I will share tangible examples of how the extremes of brain behaviors show up in leadership styles, and from which brain hemisphere, theoretically, these extremes have likely developed. I will explain this as a theoretical yet life-applicable concept. For example, how does over-emphasis on left-brain styles versus right-brain styles manifest in the way we act at the office? I will also paint a picture of how a more balanced style shows up in an effective leader. How much assertiveness or empathy you show as an individual is up to you when you operate at higher levels of self-mastery. Being hijacked by office drama is a consequence of not understanding how to direct and manage your own thoughts, feelings, and emotions, as well as your intention/attention. Wherever you are is where you begin. This is a lifelong process of development.

At this point, we are ready to take the Leadership Self-Evaluation. Don't analyze yourself or the statements; just go with "your gut." Don't overthink your choices. This should be done quickly and spontaneously.

LEADERSHIP SELF-EVALUATION

Valencia Ray, M.D.

Instructions:

In each of the numbered sets of statements, circle one letter (A, B, or C) to indicate the statement that most accurately reflects your general leadership style. After making your choices, calculate your score according to the directions at the end of the evaluation.

1. A. You know what is best and expect that those you lead will trust your authority.
    B. You prefer consensus, even if it means a lack of closure at staff meetings.
    C. You encourage others to "make their voices heard" by providing explicit agreements for group engagement.

2. A. Your decision-making is based on how you feel about things, regardless of precedent.
   B. Your decision making is based on input from others and traditional indicators as well as your intuition for innovation.
   C. Your decision-making is based solely on rational ideas that are based on past performance.

3. A. You are people-focused; relationships typically matter more than results.
   B. You are results driven, task focused, and tend toward impatience with things that interfere with your desired outcomes.
   C. You are relationship focused and empathetic; yet you will expediently move to reassign people who are not getting the job done.

4. A. You value avoidance of conflict over process and structure when pursuing goals.
   B You have a vision and have the people skills to inspire others to venture into the unknown due to your clarity, consistency, and ability to influence others.
   C. You value hard work to reach goals over relationship building.

5. A. Control, predictability, and order are vitally important to you.
   B. You go with the flow; order is not particularly important to you.
   C. You are adaptable and have a reputation for having a clear, process-centered focus as unexpected change occurs.

6. A. You tend to lose track of deadlines and often lack follow through.
   B. You tend to have orderly, clear deadlines that you strive to reach; yet, you are flexible enough to course correct when needed.
   C. You are driven to do things better and faster, and you will take over a situation to forge ahead quickly.

7. A. Time is of the essence to you; you expect people to "just do it right" and dislike having to slow down to clarify process, values, and desired outcome details.

    B. You create group dynamics that allow for trust and clarity of personal and organizational values, while being cognizant of conciseness and time constraints.

    C. It is important for you to be very patient with people who lack confidence and need extra hand-holding, even if it takes a lot of time.

8. A. You prefer self-help programs that deal with our "inner world" and feelings.

    B. You prefer personal and professional development programs that deal with business skill set and mindset transformation.

    C. You avoid "touchy-feely" training and development programs.

9. A. You believe people need to ignore their below-the-surface personality issues; leave them at home and "just get on with it" at the office.

    B. You believe that people need to talk out their feelings with co-workers as these feelings arise.

    C. You believe that self-awareness of emotional management and intellectual skill set development is vital to a healthy and productive organization.

10. A. Your tendency is to listen, though you may not include the ideas of all stakeholders in the group before giving a final directive.

    B. You believe that the leader should not have to deal with ideas and opinions that differ from his or her vision.

    C. You tend to include all of the ideas and opinions of team members with a goal of reaching consensus before making a final decision.

Results Instructions

In the **key** below, circle in each style (I, II, and III) the numbered letter (e.g., 1A, 1B, or 1C) that matches the statement choice you made above. Then add up the number of responses in each style group and write that total in the box below that corresponds to each style.

Example of how to determine the total number of your responses. As you can see from the number of **BOLD** responses, this example is predominantly a Style I:

Style I: **1A, 2C, 3B,** 4C, **5A,** 6C, **7A,** 8C, **9A, 10B**

Style II: 1B, 2A, 3A, 4A, 5B, 6A, 7C, 8A, 9B, 10C

Style III: 1C, 2B, 3C, **4B,** 5C, **6B,** 7B, **8B,** 9C, 10A

(Tally: Style I = 7, Style II = 0, and Style III = 3)

Key:

Style I: 1A, 2C, 3B, 4C, 5A, 6C, 7A, 8C, 9A, 10B

Style II: 1B, 2A, 3A, 4A, 5B, 6A, 7C, 8A, 9B, 10C

Style III: 1C, 2B, 3C, 4B, 5C, 6B, 7B, 8B, 9C, 10A

Style I. Commanding Style (Left-Dominant)	Style II. Social-Overdrive (Right-Dominant)	Style III. Collaborative Style (Integrated Style)
Total =	Total =	Total =

Now that you have an understanding of the three primary styles, what's next? Throughout this book, we've seen that we are capable of re-wiring our beliefs, attitudes, and behaviors, using our entire brain to be the best leaders we can possibly be. Now that you have a sense of where your tendencies are as a leader, let's explore what it looks like to adapt in the areas where you tend towards a style that is "too cold" or "too hot." You then can better determine what is, "just right" for you.

Key Points

- Our personal leadership tendencies ultimately form the culture of our companies and organizations.

- Without knowing your starting point, reaching your destination will be challenging at best.

- Culture impacts employee levels of productivity and performance.

- There is a strong tendency for people to believe that their profile is "who they are;" often, this is not the case. Our profile is more often, 'who you think you are,' and it reflects how you currently show up in life. This evolves.

- Leaders and their team members will need to grow personally and professionally in order to improve their communication skills, emotional intelligence, and develop the willingness to keep learning and evolving new technical skill sets.

- In the same way that we want to integrate and use the whole brain, the innovative company integrates both traditional and collaborative structures.

- Leadership structures provide support for the leadership style.

- Each style has its own nuances that can be more effective in a given situation. The key here is level of flexibility and range.

- The transition of cultures from hierarchy with command-control styles to a structure of collaboration with cooperative leadership styles is the challenge leaders currently face.

- As leaders become more confidently self-aware and resilient, they will be able to see beyond a narrow focus and broaden that focus to include the much-needed development of the people within the company.

- We are capable of rewiring our beliefs, attitudes and behaviors, using our entire brains to be the best leaders we can possibly be.

Reflection: Inquiring Mind

1. How would you define the structure of the leadership model for your organization?

2. Does it support innovation and team engagement? Why or why not?

3. In your present organization, which leadership style do you think is most effective? Why?

4. If your current organization is struggling with team engagement and productivity, how do you think the current leadership structure should be modified?

5. As a leader, in what ways do you think your organization's culture is impacted by the current leadership styles that predominate?

Envision Possibilities

1. What do you envision as the ideal leadership structure for your current organization's purpose and mission?

2. What would a training program look like that would address leadership style, team engagement and culture in a holistic, sustainable way? Can you identify the people that should be involved and how active learning (real life application) could be integrated into the everyday workplace?

3. How would individual levels of self-awareness impact the feasibility of changing leadership structures, styles and culture?

CHAPTER SEVEN

PORTRAYALS OF LEADERSHIP STYLES

*The world is a looking glass and gives back to every man
the reflection of his own face.*

— William M. Thackeray

To be most effective, the leader will need to evolve self-awareness (his or her own as well as the team's), and allow the team to engage more directly with the organization's vision, purpose, values, strategy, and outcomes. Using an explicit communication style can support these objectives. This requires more clarity and transparency, which is a growth challenge for most leaders. The leader must be willing to take a look in the mirror *and* be willing to evolve him or herself. The organization's environment and culture is a reflection of leadership style. People form the culture, and the culture reinforces future behavior. Hopefully, the pressure to change is strong enough now to give leaders the incentive to stop avoiding the unavoidable. Evolution never stops; change is a constant. Using hierarchical structure as a disguise for a command-control style—which is an extremely individualistic style—squashes innovation, group participation, and individual employee growth. *Command-control uses hierarchy in a way that subverts communication because it creates an atmosphere of mistrust and fear.* It also creates environments that are stressful.

This chapter is about becoming more conscious of behaviors— and identifying as whether they are based in "individualism" or "collaboration." Individualistic tendencies are reflected by the left-brain point of view, while the collaborative engages both the left and right-brain hemispheres and is more holistic. As a reference point, I have also offered a theoretical view of what extreme left-brain and extreme right-brain lateralization would look like behaviorally. These descriptions are detailed later in this chapter. It was from these traits that the evaluation tool noted in the previous chapter was developed. Using an analogy based in the well-known childhood story about the three bears, the extreme left-brain could be considered "too hot;" the extreme right-brain "too cold," and the collaboration between hemispheres would be "just right." Because we are aware of how brain hemisphere qualities impact behavior, we can do exercises to help "retrain" our brains. Self-awareness is the first and very important step to real personal and professional transformation.

As an example, if talking too much and not listening to others is a challenge for you (a strong left-brain issue since the left-brain is verbal and action-oriented), doing exercises that increase empathy, reflection, and receptivity such as listening (a function of the right-brain) could help to balance your leadership tendency. Recognizing your behaviors helps to accelerate self-awareness regarding the root of the problem. Once the root of the problem is brought to awareness, you can then use targeted practice exercises and tools to help master the challenge at hand, then applying your learning to real life situations. Of course, there could be deep cellular memories to account for why a "part of you" needs to be heard so much and why you are a poor listener. As was discussed in previous chapters, the deepest roots tend to be in the "subconscious mind." One need not dive this deeply into self-discovery until ready to go there; but in the meantime, having the brain awareness to recognize the source of behavior can be a strategic advantage for directing behavior modification exercises into the everyday workplace. From a traditional perspective, even addressing leadership behavior challenges at this minimal level is a quantum leap. Historically, workplace training was only focused on giving people tactical transactional tools; not on self-knowledge. As people become more self-aware, they can address the "blind spots" that prevent them from applying their tactical skills or limit them from engaging with their work from their hearts.

When we embrace the concept that we are not "fixing" our "self" but instead "learning and growing to reach our true potential," we can more easily access and remove our blind spots from our Mind's Eye. The workplace environment then becomes a place of "productive productivity," and people can look forward to enjoying their work instead of dreading it. A happy, contributing employee or team member is a more effective, efficient, and healthier employee. It offers a win-win for all parties concerned, including the organizations and the shareholders. It is a sustainable and profitable model for the long run and contributes to a more stable economy and society.

EXPANDING OUR LEADERSHIP VISION

As I pointed out in the previous chapter, collaborative leadership is an innovation to the hierarchical model but is not the same as consensus. The collaborative leadership structure requires higher levels of self-awareness than most people have currently developed, in large part because of past conditioning. A majority of people are too self-protective and on hyper-alert for conflict to spontaneously move to a collaborative culture. Paradoxically, as I have mentioned, since the brain "finds what you keep your attention on," you will always find drama and conflict if you expect drama and conflict, or you think that people need constant monitoring and must be told what to do. It is not that we are incapable of operating at higher levels of awareness; we just haven't had enough brain awareness or clarity of intention to move consistently toward this paradigm. People need to genuinely be heard, to get their "voices in the room," and feel that they can make a contribution without fear of being treated with disrespect. People are looking for more autonomy, self-mastery, and purpose for their own lives; they should not be reserved for the CEO alone.

As long as the terms of how people will engage in team meetings are explicit, and team conflict is dealt with methodically by training and implementation, a culture of trust and vulnerability can be created to support collaboration. As you can imagine, this takes a healthy degree of self-awareness on the part of all team members. And it is the reason that the workplace is so ideal for personal growth and development. A wise application of neuroscience can definitely accelerate this process. I have made this discovery personally in my own life; it is not simply a theoretical concept. By integrating personal development within the context of addressing team dysfunction and doing it within the framework of real-life workplace projects and experiences, we can see change that will endure. This is the only way to create sustainable, real-time change. Quick fix weekend seminars or a one-day offsite seminar are only patchwork approaches that have poor track records historically.

It should also be clear that the new personal development skills learned at the office could be applied to daily personal life as well. The person who does this as a way to improve overall health and well-being would not only have more energy at work, he or she could also use the new skills to create a healthy lifestyle in general. This is what I witnessed within my own medical practice. Employees often shared with me how what they were learning at work was making their overall life more enjoyable. Specifically, they were making better relationship choices, finding the time and discipline to take better care of their bodies, and raising their self-confidence. As brain research continues to support the importance of "right-brain" engagement and its benefits, we will likely create new paradigms for lifestyles that are more effective and healthier for society as a whole. This too becomes part of our challenge since our social structures are also too inflexible. *Too much emphasis is put on how much time one spends at the office instead of how effective and efficient one is.* If an employee is able to plan and complete the work on time, why fill the additional time with more busy work? As Colin Powell described in his autobiographical book, *It Worked for Me: In Life and Leadership*, being a "busy bastard" is not the path to high levels of productivity, health, or life fulfillment.

We are making a transition and we are learning; hence, there is a learning curve. To the degree that people are coming from a place of alignment around values, purpose, and mission, this transition period is much more likely to be successful when crossing into the new world of collaborative leadership. The mind and heart must be engaged. I have already established that our cognitive behavior is not hardwired. To the degree that we embrace this fact, we can more easily address our gaps. We can then create leadership development plans with clarity, integrating our values into our goals and objectives. There is no one-size-fits-all way of leadership that works in all settings. As Richard Fairbank, CEO at Capital One puts it,

Finding a visionary strategy you believe in as a leader is a very intuitive thing. There are many things a leader can't predict using data.

LEARNING TO FLOURISH

Jim Collins, author of *Good to Great*, suggests four basic practices for creating a culture that supports internal motivation and helps employees to flourish:

1. Lead with questions, not answers.

2. Engage in dialogue and debate, not coercion.

3. Conduct autopsies, without blame.

4. Build "red flag" mechanism[s]. In other words, create a culture where is it safe to explicitly express ideas and observations regarding identified problems.

Notice, however, that these four practices are not currently the norm. There must be a culture of collaboration and trust to support these ideas. As Gallup and others, such as the Towers Watson 2012 Global Workforce Study reveal, employee disengagement levels are running as high as nearly 70%. While defining leadership as "authoritarian" may have worked in the past industrial age, we are in a new age where people do not tolerate well only being told coercively what to do. Our survival mindset needs to be upgraded to an intention to thrive, to flourish. Flourishing engages the mind and heart by integrating values, purpose, and mission into the culture. *By helping people to become explicit about their own personal values and purpose and how these intercept with the organization's values and purpose, a sense of connection is made between the employees and the company.* When people feel that they are a part of something greater than themselves, and feel the bond of a community, loyalty and productivity dramatically increase. Of course, this can be measured with objective, financial metrics as well. Employee engagement is not only cost-effective; companies that are known for engagement tend to be ranked as the best places to work. These companies also tend to be purpose-driven organizations. A 2008 Towers Perrin Global Workforce Study of 50 companies over a one year period correlated their employee engagement levels with their financial results. The companies with high employee engagement had a 19% increase in operating income and almost a 28% growth in earnings per share. Conversely, companies with low levels of engagement saw operating income drop more than 32% and earnings per share decline over 11%. If we want cultures of innovation and adaptability, we need new terms of engagement for leaders and teams.

ON MOTIVATION

Motivation is not carrots and sticks. If a task is tedious, routine, and unimaginative, carrots and sticks may work, but technology increasingly is assuming these tasks. Especially given employee cynicism about "authority figures," motivation needs to be internally driven in this age of innovation, non-routine work, and rapid change. It is inspiration that will give rise to action that is truly productive and sustainable. Inspiration comes from within the individual. Leaders who are confident enough to be vulnerable and authentic are more likely to inspire the best from their team members. This breeds a culture of trust and loyalty as well. When people feel visible and cared for, they are more likely to be inspired to give the organization their best. It is also time to close the gap between the myth of gender behavior and what motivates people. When we as leaders can motivate and inspire based on the needs of the person in front of us (instead of a caricature of what a man or woman "should" need), we will become more effective.

In general, I think it is safe to say that people increasingly expect more from their work. We need a triple bottom-line proposition of People, Planet, and Profits, an increasingly popular idea within business circles. Making the workplace an environment that enriches people's personal and professional lives will motivate beyond all expectations at times. I know; I witnessed this with my own employees. The results can be remarkable.

Engaged employees generate 43% more revenue than disengaged employees (Hay Group, 2001). Engaged employees are, quite simply, much less likely to leave. We all know that employee turnover is expensive. With high levels of engagement, firms can realize a revenue growth of 2.5 times that of their peers and reduce expensive staff turnover by 40%. (Hay Group, 2010). According to Gallup, disengagement costs $300 billion in lost productivity and employee performance over a five-year period (or $60 billion per year). As you can see, there are benefits to developing "soft skills."

Is your leadership style, "too hot, too cold or just right" in a given situation or for your organizational culture? If not, how can you adjust it?

We need to ask ourselves these questions without deferring to the age-old idea that our behavior is "just the way we are," or blaming it on gender. As a leader, if you are not willing to change and your organization needs to change in order to thrive, then perhaps it is a better idea to find an organizational culture for which you are better suited.

BRAIN TRAIT EXAMPLES

I have divided the "leadership brain behaviors" into three categories. The "Extreme Left-brain Style" is how I would define Command-Control. The polar opposite of the extremely individualistic left-brained Command-Control style is what I would refer to as the Social Overdrive style. The Social Overdrive style of leadership is ineffectively focused on the relationship between the leader and others. The leader may be so "visionary" that he or she is not grounded or able to take action. Or—the leader may be such a "people pleaser" that he or she cannot hold people accountable. The Social Overdrive style reflects a focus on the extreme right-brain traits without the tempering effects of the left-brain. You can refer to my chart on hemisphere differences presented in chapter four for a review of these "brain traits." The Collaborative Style represents integration of the two hemispheres in a way that is situational and more effective. It is dynamic instead of rigid, reactive or robotic.

The examples that follow concern behaviors that show up when one's pattern of leadership behavior is extremely dominant to either brain hemisphere. I also indicate, theoretically, what a balance between the two hemispheres would look like. I based these categorizations upon the qualities that research has ascribed to the two hemispheres. Please keep in mind, however, that the operating system of our brain is very complex. What follows is a simplified way of communicating for business purposes. We need a working model, however, in order to organize our discussion. There are some staunch scientists who cannot see the forest for the trees and will argue over minute details. As I explained in the beginning of this book, my presentation of the science is in a colloquial style that allows for simplicity and real-life application. This is a model intended to be understood and used by the general public. Hard-core basic science often does not accomplish this goal.

As previously noted, the left-brain characteristics historically have been considered "male," and the right-brain characteristics "female." Of course, this is stereotyping because both genders have access to both brain hemispheres if deliberately practiced. Also, gender behavior is actually a spectrum and not a "written in stone," genetically hardwired pattern. It is not my intention to create yet another set of categories for "leadership styles;" however, as mentioned, for the purpose of organization and structure, I have divided leadership behavioral styles into three categories. By emphasizing extremes, it is easier to discern the differences between the brain-hemispheres and then adjust according to authentic personality preference and the needs of the organization's culture. In light of this, please note that the following portrayals are drawn from "typical" qualities associated with the given hemisphere and are not intended to imply that the hemispheres act totally independent of each other.

I. Extreme Left-Brain Style

Command-Control or Task Driven

- Overtly narcissistic tendencies

- Too much intellect; too little heart

- Pushy and bossy communication style

- Poor listening skills

- Prone to distorting the truth without empathy

- Task oriented and goal-driven with impatience

- Hyperactive without real clarity of vision

- Overly analytical

- Poor people skills

- Insensitive to other people; too self-protective

- Seeing others as threatening or antagonistic in general

II. Extreme Right-Brain Style

Social Overdrive Style

- "People pleaser"

- Too much heart; not enough boundaries

- Fear of confrontation

- Scattered and unfocused

- High on expressing feelings without the container to direct them productively

- Overly sympathetic (not the same as empathy)*

- Laxity in results due to inadequate feedback guidance and need to "be nice"

- Excessive consensus

- Idealistic without viable structure or plan

*Sympathy and empathy are often confused. Sympathy is overly associating with the feelings of others, whereas empathy is a willingness to be non-judgmental as well as a willingness to seek to understand another's viewpoint or circumstance, even though one may not have direct experience with that viewpoint or circumstance. Empathy allows for the other to feel validated without the empathetic person necessarily having to agree with the other's point-of-view.

III. Collaborative Brain Style

Situation-Based Leadership, Adaptable/Flexible Styles

- Not defensive; willing to be vulnerable

- Comfortable with self

- Adaptable to change

- Inspires others to engage when facing change

- Relates to people in context, professionally and appropriately — empathetically

- Drives and inspires team members' personal and professional development

- Encourages open, direct and honest communication, tempered with sensitivity

- Visionary; influential with clear directives and processes

- Balance of intellect and emotion/feeling intelligences

- Explicit communication style engaging dialogue

- Good listening skills with authenticity

- Goal focused, while engaging the hearts of team members

- Responds instead of reacts

Now that you have a sense of where your natural tendencies as a leader might be, let's explore what it looks like to adapt in the areas where you tend towards a style that is "too cold" or "too hot." The more self-aware we are of what drives our behavior choices, the easier it is to change these behaviors. Also, getting in touch with our own values and purpose allows for more passionate alignment with certain styles rather than with others. This is not about conforming yourself to a culture; it's about authentically developing your own true potential. Then, as a leader, you can either contribute to cultural change or find another environment where you can thrive. Sometimes this is necessary in order for you to grow and develop.

EXAMPLE PROFILES FOR PRACTICAL APPLICATION

The following are examples of each brain style and are constructed from profiles of clients. The examples provided are based on composites of actual individuals for whom I have provided executive coaching services. Of course, the names and specific personal details have been changed for reasons of privacy. I will provide a situation analysis (prior state), objectives (future state), and basic tactics and key lessons learned. The next chapter, chapter eight, will offer more detailed tools and exercises for your own application in order to accelerate your personal transformation.

Example One

John was a senior executive leader who was known to have poor listening skills. He often disregarded input from the leaders within his team. He was perceived as intimidating and as a "know-it-all." In fact, he discouraged debate between himself and others and used his authority to shut others down. He often did not fully understand the scope of company issues because he didn't take the time to gather information from his leaders or from his employees on the front lines. He was quick to take action and did not value reflection, dialogue, or engaging others in strategic visioning. He was overly focused on "looking good" and managing up. While this may have garnered him promotions in the past, he was now situated in a more complex position and had not developed sufficient leadership skill at his new, more senior level. His lack of relationship savvy was starting to derail his leadership team's effectiveness. They complained that they felt like cogs in a wheel, just going through the motions, and that their talents were not being appreciated or cultivated for professional growth. The resulting general atmosphere had no sense of purpose or community and generated feelings that the executive leader was only interested in his own self-promotion. Meetings lacked clarity, and mistrust and lack of vulnerability were rampant. People were very guarded in their behavior. Productivity was dropping rapidly; the department was beginning to be less efficient and appeared disorganized as silos proliferated.

What leadership style do you think is exhibited by this example? If you were thinking "Extreme Left-brain" behavior, you are correct. The left-brain is what makes us "individualistic." It helps our sense of ego-self to create boundaries between oneself and others. It is also concerned with taking care of our external 3D world survival needs. If we are too focused on competition as a workplace paradigm, the left-brain will really activate our competitive tendencies and exacerbate our insecurities. The left-brain is also the verbal hemisphere, which loves to talk and is focused more on taking action. People who talk too much and do not listen are tapping extensively into their left-brain qualities without the balance of receptivity from the right-brain. Additionally, the lack of empathy and poor relationship skill, as well as the lack of a sense of community purpose, is illustrative of one who is too focused on the left-brain. Left-brain extreme is exemplified by rugged individualism or "Lone Ranger" tendencies. It is not people-focused in a connected way. It tends to see people as a means to an isolated end goal. The lack of clarity also is an indication that vision and intention have not been identified and articulated. Clarity of vision is a quality of the right hemisphere, which thinks in images and contextualizes in terms of the big picture. The left-brain, on the other hand, focuses more on tactics and "pieces;" it relies on past "logic." Short-term piecemeal thinking is common. The left-brain is uncomfortable with feelings and the unknown. It represses feelings and relies on intellect and its own form of "logic."

This leader would benefit first from realizing how his behavior is handicapping him as a leader. The 21st century leader will need to possess empathy and have good people skills. When the meaning of empathy is reframed as a strength, and "The Science of Feelings" is explained in a way that connects empathy with real improvement in personal and professional performance, it will receive more attention. It also has been shown that empathy, an important ingredient in people skill, improves the financial bottom line. There are many incentives for raising one's level of empathy. With the willingness to evolve, exercises to "make friends with feelings" alongside emotional intelligence skill development, can have a great impact on the leader's personal growth and development. These skills can also reduce stress, help to cultivate trust and open communication, and lead to tangible engagement of purpose and values. As a leader becomes more attuned to others, he or she can engage a sense of teamwork and community. This will help retain high-performing employees as well. Also, neuroscience-based exercises can be developed to help the leader with confidence so that he or she is comfortable receiving feedback, information, and support from others. Often, people who are "know-it-all's" are insecure at some level and hide behind the mask of authority. This is not right or wrong; it is simply not the best way to gain respect and loyalty from others and evolve to more effective behavior. Others need to have opportunities for healthy self-expression as well. Remember, this is not about fixing yourself; it is about expanding your leadership vision. The leader in this example would do well to learn how to:

1. Listen

2. Ask questions instead of "telling" (Or talking too much)

3. Reflect on the needs of others who wish to contribute in meaningful ways

4. Slow down to clarify his purpose, goals, and strategic vision for his team and be willing to receive input to create ownership and alignment that will engage others

5. Learn Neuroscience 101 so he can understand how his perception and focus are actually derailing him and to find ways to better self-manage and evolve his mindset blind spots

Fast forward. As this leader became more self-aware and accepting of his leadership gaps, he was able to listen more effectively without cutting people off, and he started to realize how helpful it was to have the insights gained from others. He also discovered that by asking questions, others responded more positively, and he learned information that was helpful to his leadership effectiveness. He came to understand that when he changed his perception from one of overt competition and the need to "control" others to showing interest in others, people were more committed to their work, and projects were completed with greater efficiency and enthusiasm. This all contributed to a more effective team and higher performance ratings.

Example Two

Sharon was a vice president of marketing and managed a team of about 60 people. She struggled with addressing conflict, and her tendency was to avoid it at all costs. She considered herself to be a peacekeeper; this behavior had served her well in the past and within the dynamics of her upbringing. She also assumed a caretaker role; not only was she the primary caretaker of her aging parents, she was also a single mom and was accustomed to putting her own needs behind others. While she was smart and ambitious, she found that it was becoming more difficult to manage people as she climbed higher up the corporate ladder. She was uncomfortable leading a team of assertive men and women, whom she often secretly found intimidating. She was beginning to realize that her lack of assertiveness was causing others to disregard her directives, and she was facing a team that seemed to be disintegrating by the month. Projects were delayed and budgets were constantly overrun. Meetings were disorganized and often hijacked by those expressing the loudest opinions. She didn't have clear objectives or agendas, and her meetings often deteriorated into painful free-for-alls.

When relationship problems were bought to her attention, she often procrastinated in addressing them, if she addressed them at all. She also was overly sensitive to feedback and was overly concerned about "hurting others' feelings." This created behavior in her that paradoxically held back her team members' development because they did not receive explicit coaching directives and were often left in the dark as to areas that needed growth and development. Team members felt undervalued, and some even attributed the lack of feedback to a lack of interest in their efforts. She found herself becoming more and more stressed and losing confidence in herself as a leader. She complained to me that her negative self-talk was overwhelming her and confided that she often felt like a fake; she wasn't feeling like a confident leader, yet she struggled to appear as if she had everything under control. She intuitively knew that there was something in the way she viewed life that was blocking her potential, but she didn't know how to define and uproot it. She was now facing scrutiny from her direct senior leader and was feeling as if she were under a microscope. She knew that a performance improvement plan was in the offing because she was informed during her review that this was underway to help her address her leadership gaps.

This leader is an example of the Social Overdrive style. She is very relationship focused but has not managed to evolve more structured skill sets, such as clarifying the strategic vision and engaging the hearts and minds of her team. She needed more structure and process mindset development. She had bought into the concept of gender stereotype when it came to "peace keeping and caretaking." She was too invested in caring for others without slowing down to rejuvenate herself or strategically clarify the objectives and desired outcomes for her department. Her disjointed team meetings reflected this. While she demonstrated empathy for others, she often became overly attached and sympathetic, which tended to blur her objectivity, decision-making, and judgment. Empathy, of course, is important to understanding the viewpoint and experience of another. When people feel understood and validated, they tend to trust and feel valued. Sympathy is a different animal; it can cause one to overlook the details and circumstances that are important to healthy boundaries and good decision-making. In reality, another reason for her sympathy was her underlying need to be liked; she feared rejection and tried to please others, keeping the peace to a fault. Sometimes this behavior has just the opposite effect; it can lead to conflict, chaos, and confusion because people lose trust when they see a leader who is inconsistent and lacks follow through.

This leader had strengths in people skills that simply needed to be organized and integrated into her personal and professional development plan. She would benefit from greater self-awareness to evolve her unconscious insecurities and her less-than-functional behavioral choices. She would need to realize that her behavior was not "just the way she is." Our defense mechanisms and behaviors are evolved over our lifetime, and cultural conditioning impacts the social context for our behaviors. As she developed her analytical skills for strategic planning, she would better understand how to enlist the strengths of those on her team to help her in this area. After all, the leader's role is not to micromanage; the ability to delegate is an important strength. Yet, one also needs to self-reflect and honestly assess one's own gaps personally and professionally in order to engage and inspire team members to commit their best efforts. As this leader learns to use her intuition and empathy in more constructive ways, she can take what she learns in terms of assertiveness, confidence, and consequential thinking to more clearly ascertain how she can cultivate and integrate the strengths of others. Also, she can inspire her team by taking the lead and having the courage to lead the way in the area of personal change and growth. The individual, the team, and the culture of the organization form a system. The best way to create an organization of innovation is to help people deal with their blind spots and better understand how to access their untapped potential through personal development. These insights then are applied in real-life opportunities to deal with others in the context of managing projects within the work place. She will thus be able to achieve a sustainable model for organizational health.

Since the environment will continue to change, the person who can embrace change without undo fear and resistance will have an advantage in today's workplace. Helping people to learn how to embrace change and innovation with greater ease is a part of the blueprint for creating a culture that supports sustainable organizational health. Emotionally intelligent, resilient leaders inspire team coherence, which is vital for real innovation and productivity. A healthy climate is not overly rigid or lax; creativity needs the container of structure and vice versa. The leader in this example would do well to:

1. Learn Neuroscience 101 so as to recognize how conditioned expectations create self-fulfilling prophecies relating to gender roles and to know how to update these conditioned expectations to a more effective "mental model"

2. Quiet her inner critic and update to more useful, less stress-provoking tactics in order to self-manage or motivate herself

3. Deepen emotional intelligence skills, including how to navigate her emotional terrain as well as how to clarify her values and purpose

4. Learn communication skills for creating engaging, collaborative, and productive team meetings

5. Develop explicit communication skills and learn exercises that support her ability to give truthful, empathetic feedback so that she can help others to grow and evolve

Fast forward. As she became aware of the tapes in her head that sabotaged her confidence, this leader was better able to speak up and share her truths at meetings, provide feedback, and avoid taking things so personally. This helped her deal with her tendency to avoid conflict. Others also began to develop greater trust and respect for her. People are always watching, and it is important for leaders to "walk their talk" and follow through on promises. As Sharon came to understand what perception is and how it determines our thoughts, feelings, and actions, she was better equipped to observe her behavior more objectively and make better choices in all areas, including within her personal life. Personal growth and "brain awareness" is transferable to every area of life. She became more productive and less stressed because she was better able to understand herself instead of comparing herself to others. This was essential to her ability to release her fear of rejection and come from her own authenticity as a leader.

Example Three

Deborah was a senior division leader of a company in the healthcare sector. She had worked her way up over the years from administrative roles to being a part of the senior leadership team. Over the years, she had to come to terms with her tendency to judge others while excusing her own behavior. Relatively early in her career, she showed signs of derailing herself by relapsing into her tendency to criticize and blame others. She tended to deflect feedback by becoming defensive or by trying to be liked and "playing up." One day, she had an epiphany that she needed to change the way she thought about herself. She had to work on her confidence so that she didn't come off as defensive when she received less than stellar feedback. She also had to overcome her insecurity about her performance ability when an opportunity for sponsorship to attend a prestigious business school materialized. Because she was willing to embrace and face her inner obstacles, she became adept at handling external obstacles as they arose. She was able to relax and accept the challenge of returning to school. As she came to see herself as a lifelong learner, she found herself evolving into a skillful team leader who was able to see others with more empathy; consequently, she became a better listener. She enthusiastically embraced the expanding knowledge base of information that helped her to understand how to proactively "retrain her brain." Her evolving confidence and personal and professional development led to better recommendations from her senior managers that boosted her career trajectory. As her team members recognized her growth and willingness to develop them and genuinely look out for their interests with the senior management team, they became very loyal, going above and beyond the call of duty. They consistently began to outperform the other divisions.

Deborah was a blend of having a focus on no-nonsense results that was balanced with taking the time to clarify her vision and business plan before leaping to action. She kept watch over the financial bottom line while at the same time developing the strengths and addressing the weaknesses of her team members, who greatly appreciated her caring attitude. She was viewed as accessible and, because of her ability to speak with truth and authenticity, she was trusted and admired. That inspired the best from those around her. How did she achieve all of this?

1. She learned to take responsibility without blaming and victimizing herself

2. She stopped excessively focusing on what others were doing wrong and started dealing her own personal and professional development blind spots

3. She began to look for the good in others and encouraged them to evolve their behaviors, thus creating a learning environment

4. She held people accountable and embraced courageous conversations

5. She kept her attention on the intended results and course-corrected as the environment shifted

Deborah is a leader who leads by example. We cannot expect others to do what we will not. Leaders must set the pace by embracing personal growth with an open mindset. The careers of most leaders are derailed because of their unwillingness to deal with their own blind spots. Remember, this is not about fixing anyone. It is about learning and growing to reach our true potential. In and of itself, this idea is novel within our current corporate environment. Instead of perpetuating denial, the engaging collaborative leader is willing to evolve himself or herself so that he or she can lead change and inspire the best from others. Leaders are learners. A growth mindset is a requirement for successful leadership in the 21st century workplace, particularly during times of turbulence and rapid change.

LEADERSHIP COMPETENCIES

Now that you have seen examples of the three brain styles, what's next? Throughout this book, we've understood that we are capable of rewiring our beliefs, attitudes, and behaviors and can use our whole brain to be the best leaders we can possibly be. However, there is also an "invisible" ingredient to success that is now coming to the forefront. And that ingredient is emotional intelligence. There are four competencies that have been identified by Lyle Spencer, an associate of David McClelland, who is known for his early work in this area of leadership development. As noted in the Goleman et al. (2002) book, *Primal Leadership*, these competencies include the following, and are exhibited by nearly all top-performing leaders:

1. Ability to take initiative

2. Possession of skills that foster collaboration and teamwork

3. Demonstrated ability to lead teams (Inspire with results)

4. Possession of the drive to achieve results

Once the requirements of an individual's basic core job training, education and skill sets are met, what separates the top performing leaders from the star pool is their level of EI (emotional intelligence) as it relates to the above competencies. This requires the ability to relate to others and adapt the style that is relevant in the moment. It also requires self-awareness and a level of self-esteem and confidence that is independent of constantly changing external influences. Self-esteem and confidence can be developed, especially when neuroscience is used in an experiential way. Of course, some business cultures support certain styles more than others; hence, "knowing one's self" is very important in selecting an environment that aligns with the leader's values and variations of style.

Getting to know one's self requires inner reflection and an ability to slow down sufficiently to re-energize and develop clarity about the invisible forces that drive our lives and organizations. This also is necessary for developing right-brain skills that allow for tapping into new ideas and implementing them in ways that are a better fit for today's environment. Current processes and systems need updating, which in turn requires developing a healthy, "intrapersonal" relationship as the foundation for higher levels of EI and leadership skill.

The next and last chapter will offer some innovative ideas and techniques for developing more self-awareness and ways of self-managing thoughts, feelings, and stress. When we decide to address ourselves as whole people, and not as a series of compartmentalized, mechanistic pieces, we can break down the silos within our minds that create the silos in the workplace and in our homes. Work/life balance begins within us. We will then have more energy and vitality as well when we come to learn how to "optimally operate" our amazing brain, on purpose, with purpose.

Key Points

- The leader must be willing to take a look in the mirror and must be willing to evolve him or her "self."

- Individualistic tendencies are reflected by the left-brain point of view, but the collaborative engages both left and right-brain hemispheres and is more holistic.

- Self-awareness is the first and most important step to real personal and professional transformation.

- When we embrace the concept that we are not "fixing" ourselves but instead "learning and growing to reach our true potential," we can more easily access and remove our blind spots from our Mind's Eye.

- Collaborative leadership is an innovation to the hierarchical model, but it is not the same as consensus.

- Collaborative leadership structure requires higher levels of self-awareness than most people have currently developed, owing mostly to our past conditioning.

- People genuinely need to be heard, to get their "voices" in the room and feel that they can make a contribution without fear of being treated with disrespect.

- It should also be clear that the new personal development skills learned at the office can be applied to daily personal life as well.

- Too much emphasis is placed on how much time one spends at the office instead of how effective and efficient one is.

- Our survival mindset needs to be upgraded to an intention to thrive, to flourish. Flourishing engages the mind and heart by integrating values, purpose and mission into the culture.

- Motivation is not carrots and sticks. If a task is tedious, routine, and unimaginative, carrots and sticks will not work.

- Leaders who are confident enough to be vulnerable and authentic are more likely to inspire the best from their team members. This creates a culture of trust and loyalty as well.

- Gender behavior is actually a spectrum, not a "written in stone" or genetically hardwired.

- Sympathy is overly associating with the feelings of others, whereas empathy is a willingness to be non-judgmental as well as a willingness to understand another's viewpoint or circumstance, even though one may not have direct experience with that viewpoint or circumstance.

- We are capable of rewiring our beliefs, attitudes, and behaviors and using our whole brain to be the best leaders we can possibly be.

- Once the requirements of an individual's basic core job training, education, and skill sets are met, what separates the top performing leaders from the star pool is their level of emotional intelligence.

- "Intrapersonal" relationship is the foundation for higher levels of EI and leadership skill.

- When we decide to address ourselves as whole people, and not as a series of compartmentalized, mechanistic pieces, we can break down the silos within our mind that create the silos in the workplace and our homes. Work/life balance begins within us.

Reflection: Inquiring Mind

1. What insights have you gained from your new awareness of "brain hemisphere styles"?

2. How does viewing personal and professional development as "learning and growing to reach more of your true potential" instead of as "fixing yourself" affect your willingness to embrace feedback and professional development opportunities?

3. What is the difference in the intention and focus of a "survival mindset" as opposed to a "thriving mindset" or flourishing mindset? How would the way that you feel during your day be impacted by these differences?

4. Does "vulnerability" mean strength or weakness to you? Do you think it requires courage to be vulnerable? Do you recognize that vulnerability doesn't mean you need to expose personal and situationally inappropriate details in the workplace?

5. What can you do to begin developing your emotional intelligence today?

Envision Possibilities

1. What would your leadership and team behavior look like if you were able to intentionally retrain your brain to support your "Ideal Future Self" leadership style?

2. Can you envision and *feel now* applying these ideas and concepts in your Mind's Eye? The key word here is "feel;" don't just daydream in your head, integrate your heart and body into it.

3. What is the mental movie for how this looks? What do you hear, see, and what are you doing and with whom? The more vivid the detail, the better your brain can co-create the situations and circumstances for you. This is how "coincidence" and synchronicity occur. What you are doing here is learning how to experience and create your life, on purpose, with purpose.

CHAPTER EIGHT

TIPS AND STRATEGIES: WHOLE BRAIN LEADERSHIP AND LIFESTYLE

There is no passion to be found playing small; in settling for a life that is less than the one you are capable of living.

— N. Mandela

L ife can be viewed as an adventure of growth, exploration, and evolution—lived with passion. As we have learned, perception creates our reality or experience of life. I know that on my quest to stop playing small and instead reach for more of my true potential, I had to change my paradigm of personal growth from "Fix to Fun," or at least see it as an acceptable and necessary part of my life. Life can be like a rollercoaster ride—thrilling or terrifying. What is the difference? Life really boils down to how you look at it; how you "see" it. If we wish to expand the vision for our lives, we need to apply the knowledge that we learn to our everyday lives. Doing this is not a quick fix, one-day event. It is a practice that takes practice.

In this chapter, I will share a few tools and exercises to help you integrate the many new insights offered in this book. It has always been my goal to make spiritual, emotional, mental, and physical development pragmatic; to do anything else is not a wise use of our time and resources.

Our resources of time, energy, and money are finite; the more we can apply new ideas and skills to real, everyday situations, the more likely it is that we will reach the life that we are capable of living. A one-size-fits-all approach does not work and, frankly, this approach has *never* really worked. We are being called to know ourselves and to align with our authentic way of being.

THE NEW ADVENTURE OF LEADERSHIP AND PERSONAL DEVELOPMENT

I am going to share five exercises in this chapter. I selected them based on the content of this book and based upon my own evolution and growth. I want to emphasize here the need to develop trust in listening to your own inner voice and guidance. What I share here, I had started applying to my life before brain research supported it, though the research continues helping me to integrate it with more understanding. How did I do this? By quieting my mind and listening to my own intuition and inner guidance. Some refer to this as "trusting your gut." I did it by intentionally and holistically cultivating the four levels of my human self—the spiritual, the emotional, the mental and the physical. I suggest you do the same. Academic researchers eventually began to use technology to apply some objectivity to the concepts I share within this book. Some even began to use language innovatively to apply catchy, memorable phrases to some of the exercise research results.

Quite frankly, much of what we are learning is ancient wisdom; it is not new. It is simply new to the Westerner's mind and to modern-day society. Now that there is objective science that supports this wisdom, it is beginning to garner more attention. I suggest that you maintain an open mind, a "growth mindset" as mentioned previously. You can use what works for you and discard the rest. Whatever you choose, practice it because, as far as the brain is concerned, taking action and repeating that action really are at the heart of learning. Also, the more enthusiastically (positive emotion) you embrace these ideas, the easier it will be for your body to move into application. Thus, it is a good idea to make learning fun or adventurous rather than something to avoid, dread, or bring you shame. It will be what you make of it. Be playful and curious. That is our power as co-creators of our experience.

EXERCISE 1: MINDFULNESS MEDITATION

I start here because it is the foundation for quieting down our hyperactive brain, which leads to our overactive lives. Mindfulness meditation is a general name for a variety of techniques which can include everything from sitting quietly in a chair or on the floor with candles glowing to simply being present and breathing mindfully while washing dishes or taking a walk. The principle to learn is that the mind is most efficient when learning in a state of calm, with open curiosity, instead of feeling anxious or thinking we already know something and have nothing to learn. There are also varying intentions or reasons for practicing meditation. For some people, it is a way to deepen spiritual awareness; for others, it is simply a way to alleviate stress. For my purposes here, within the context of this book, I am sharing mindfulness meditation as a means for accelerating personal and professional growth and development. We must begin to increase our self-awareness as leaders and to tap more of the qualities of the right-brain hemisphere and Level 3 Thrival brain, which include greater emotional intelligence skills, self-management of feelings, and ways to expand our innovative and creative capacities. Our right-brain has deeper connections to our emotional brain than does the left-brain; therefore, it is more comfortable dealing with feelings than the left-brain. Mindfulness is a consistent way to increase self-awareness and cultivate right-brain qualities.

189

Meditation is also central to reducing stress, which is now at epidemic levels and very damaging to our physical, cognitive, and social/emotional health. Neuroscience research, healthcare data, and management studies support the need to reduce stress. Fear and worry lead to stress. A stressed and overwhelmed employee is more likely to have increased absenteeism and lower productivity. The 2012 data generally reveals that:

- 98% of employers who measure employee well-being say stress is a workforce issue. (Towers Watson HR Consulting, UK)

- Employees who feel burned out develop heart problems at a 79% higher rate than less stressed out workers. (Tel Aviv University)

- 65% of workers cite work as a significant source of stress. (American Psychological Assn.)

Burnout is a colloquial phrase that accurately describes what happens when there is over-activity without restoration. Even machines can "burn out" if improperly and overly used. Our minds can face the same type of malfunction.

The principle at work here is to slow down your busy brain waves. There are four basic brain waves that relate to this discussion:

1. Beta (14–30 Hz)—The busy, chattering mind

2. Alpha (8–13.9 Hz)—The present, reflective mind, more aware of surroundings and feelings

3. Theta (4–7.9 Hz)—Deeply relaxed; can access even deeper self-awareness/unconscious. (However, for most people it means falling asleep)

4. Delta (.1–3.9 Hz)—A sleep pattern in general

Most people live in the Beta range. This is where we experience the most stress or get distracted and lost in negative self-talk. Chronically remaining in Beta state is toxic to your brain and body. This level also does not support learning or high-level decision making because it tends to block your "gut" or intuitive insights. And, it can lead to mental and emotional fatigue and burn out.

In order to calm your feelings and stress response so that you can apply your emotional intelligence skills, you will first need to quiet this Beta noise. Mindfulness meditation practice is *not* an "acute" emotional intelligence tool; it supports the application of EI skills. Developing mindfulness allows you to develop quieting-on-demand ability for the long-term. In fact, with diligent application and practice, you can live more routinely in the Alpha state in your everyday life. Then you can be "calm, cool, and collected" in the midst of chaos. You will be able to access the Level 3 Thrival brain on demand so that you can make better decisions, be more empathetic, and create better human relationship connections. You can also imagine and create a more expanded vision for your life, once you develop the mind muscle of your Level 3 brain. This is how I want you to understand the tool of mindfulness; it is foundational to brain integration, making change easier and more lasting. It is key to breaking free from the tyranny of your Level 1 and 2 conditioned brain. It is the way to keep from simply living robotically or allowing your Level 1 and 2 brain to keep you in states of fear, being hyper-alert to unfounded threat and feeling separated and isolated from your fellow human beings. This has implications for both your professional and personal life.

I also want to point out that slowing down your brain waves does not make you less ambitious or lazy. There is a myth that being mindful means losing one's drive or motivation for performance or success. I have found mindfulness to have just the opposite effect. I tend to be clearer, less stressed, more purposeful and effective, and much more strategic and

efficient. This has led to greater enthusiasm and drive because I am energized—drawn forward and empowered by a clearer vision rather than
pushed or driven by fear of failure or a habitual state of being too busy for
busyness sake.

Also, be aware that mindfulness meditation has a host of benefits beyond the few I have already stated. There are many general health and
positive side effects as well as other cognitive benefits. These can include:
strengthening your immune system and emotional calm as well as increasing your memory capacity and ability to learn.

How do you do this? The following are three techniques based on my
own experience and the experience of some of my clients.

Technique One

This first technique is for those of you who are so hyperactive that you
can't sit still for more than a minute before your mind starts badgering
you about your to-do list. It is for those who find it too challenging to sit
longer than 5 minutes because the chatter begins to overwhelm them. This
technique requires that you simply invest in a stereo audio track of sound
that entrains your brain waves, known as "brainwave synchronization." It
operates just as a tuning fork that can entrain or pick up the vibration of
another fork across the room. It will have the effect of slowing down your
Beta state to a more relaxed Alpha state. Once you have had some practice
and are better able slow down your thoughts, you can simply learn how
to focus your attention on your own without the use of external means.
(I can recommend an inexpensive product CD I used over ten years ago
that is still available online or can be purchased from major book retailers).
All you would need are stereo-headphones and a music playback device.
You can start with the Alpha system and progress to the Theta Relaxation
system. Both the Alpha and Theta CD soundtracks that I've used in the
past are by Dr. Jeffery Thompson.

Technique Two

Another technique is to focus on your breath or on a short word or phrase. Deep, slow breathing attunes your body to your parasympathetic nervous system—the part of your nervous system that causes you to relax. This keeps your mind focused and will quiet the chatter running through your mind. Quieting the mind has the effect of reducing the stress response in your body as well. Herbert Benson, MD, introduced this idea to the academic and business world as early as the 1970s in his book, *The Relaxation Response.* He demonstrated how meditation was just as effective as medication in reducing high blood pressure—without the costs or side effects. Fortunately, this information is now beginning to receive the attention it deserves, thanks to recent advances in neuroscience. As you quiet your mind, your mind becomes clearer and is able to make space for reflection and insights, including new creative ideas and ways to implement them. You will be better able to access the executive level of your brain/mind for a higher level of strategic planning. You can be more effective and less stressed. The following are some simple guidelines for you as you begin your practice:

1. Decide before beginning whether you will choose to focus on a word, phrase, or simply your breath.

2. Your goal is not to resist or fight against the mental chatter; in an attitude of non-judgment, simply think of your thoughts as drifting clouds or brain waves rolling in and out of your mind and focus your attention back onto your breath or the word/phrase.

3. Sit quietly in a comfortable position with your eyes closed.

4. Relax each major group of muscles in your body by scanning each area with an intention to release tension. For example, focus on your shoulders, inhale while raising your shoul-

ders up to your ears with a big contraction (squeezing the muscles) of your neck and shoulder muscles, followed by an equal-sized exhale to match the inhaled breath, while releasing muscle tension in your neck and shoulders and lowering your shoulders. Slowly rotating your shoulders forward and backwards in equal amounts can also be helpful. You can also contract and release your buttocks, thighs, calves and toes, inhaling when you contract and exhaling when you release. Feeling your feet on the ground helps to increase awareness of your body. We are often too focused in our head, so to speak, and this can contribute to muscle tension in our body that leads to unhealthy shallow breathing patterns.

5. Another way to begin is to simply inhale for a count of four and exhale for a count of four. You don't have to be precise in the number count; the point is to take even, deliberate deep breaths. Set your intention on not worrying about "getting it right."

6. Assume an observer's attitude; if they do, notice thoughts floating by and then return your focus to your breath or word/phrase.

7. Practice for 5 minutes and build up to 20 minutes per sitting. First thing early in the morning and about an hour before bedtime would be ideal. Doing this in the evening also will help you to relax so as to increase the likelihood of sound sleep.

8. Gradually return your attention to the room and open your eyes before standing. Gradually stand; it is not a good idea to abruptly end your session.

To conclude, you can then make notes in your journal or pause to reflect on your experience. The more you can be intentional with your practice and process your insights, the faster your brain can begin to integrate mindfulness into your everyday ritual or habit.

Technique Three

The third and last method for beginning to acquaint yourself with mindfulness is by listening to a guided meditation. I have provided a guided meditation here as a practical example. You can record it in your own voice and simply listen to it. It is only about a 5 – 7 minute exercise. This meditation is meant to help you to see your "Self" as separate from your thoughts. I have also added language at the end to help you connect your strategic planning and visioning into your relaxation practice. These are merely tips and suggestions.

I would call the process of imaging a desired outcome as *visioning* instead of *mindfulness meditation*. Mindfulness meditation is quieting the mind to reduce thought. Once the mind is quiet, this makes the visioning more effective and more likely to become a part of your subconscious mind. Also, adding a feeling sensation makes the vision more real to the brain and nervous system. Visioning is best done in an alpha or theta brain wave state because it also facilitates your subconscious mind to help you gain insights on how to materialize your desired outcomes. Envisioning and making clear positive affirmation statements in your mind, or speaking the affirmations quietly while in this relaxed state, is very useful to the creative process. I like to refer to this as "visioning by design" (on purpose, instead of haphazardly). This is a way to direct your thoughts and intentions on purpose instead of just allowing your mind to ramble on with those 60,000 thoughts per day mentioned in a previous chapter.

To begin this meditation, simply follow steps 1 – 4 outlined in the previous technique and begin listening to the following script. Dr. Daniel

Siegel, who is a neuroscientist and psychiatrist with areas of study that include attachment theory and mindfulness, inspired the idea for this script. At the end, I also added ideas for you to note regarding ways to apply guided visualization in the business and leadership context. The ocean is commonly used as a metaphor for our mind, our subconscious, and even our feelings; it is often the source of relaxation for me in my life. I often meditate or relax to the sounds of rolling ocean waves. Let us begin:

It is empowering to become aware of your own mind. Our life keeps us too busy and we tend to ignore taking conscious control of our awareness. We are going to take a couple of minutes to do just that. Begin by sitting straight in your chair, with feet planted flat on the floor. Keep your eyes open and let your attention focus across the room. Move your attention to the center of the room. Move it to your lap. Notice how you can move your attention at will.

Now, with your eyes closed, focus on your chest. Continue to breathe slowly and deeply. Inhale and exhale at an equal, slow, and deep pace. Now focus on your feet. Focus on your breath as it moves in and out of your nose. Notice the rise and fall of your chest or stomach as you breathe. Choose a comfortable location to notice your breathing and use this as your focal point. It can be your nostrils, your chest, or abdomen . . . or just noticing your whole body as breathing.

Whenever you notice that your mind has drifted . . . to your e-mail, to what you need to do, to a worry, to an old memory, just notice it without any judgment and move your attention back to your breath or point of focus. (Pause).

As you are relaxing and following your breath, I'm going to share with you an ancient metaphor.

The mind is like the ocean. From deep in the ocean, it is tranquil and still. Even if there is turbulence on the surface, if you go deep enough, it all quiets down. The waves roll in and out on the surface, and sometimes they even crash against the shore. This is like our mind. You can think of your brain waves like the waves on the surface of the ocean. On the surface, there is often noise and chatter—turbulence. But as we relax and go deeper, we can start to notice the turbulence at the surface without being disturbed or drawn into the back and forth brain wave movements. The brain waves that cause excessive thoughts, feelings, or even old memories may float by, but just watch them as an observer, like waves rolling in and out from the shore. These thoughts are at the surface. Each time you notice these waves, bring your attention back to your breath and enjoy the peacefulness you may feel in your mind and body.

Notice that you are separate from your thoughts, meaning that the thoughts are not "YOU" as a person; they are brain waves, rolling in and out of focus. The totality of you is much more than rolling brain waves. They are simply a part of the experience of your mind. Some may be labeled as thought, some as feelings, and some as chatter or stories; just notice with awareness and bring your attention back to your breath without judging them.

While we are in this state, we can also choose to focus our attention on a question for which we need an answer. We can reflect and ponder and receive intuitive insight in this state. We can imagine our 'Ideal Self' and new behaviors. We can imagine what our new business will look like, or achieving some important outcome that will improve our leadership performance or sales results. The imagination is often the preview to real circumstances that will occur in your life with focused intention. You can also focus on positive affirmations with positive feelings of gratitude to increase the likelihood of rewiring your brain for these new results. Keep your attention on your breath for just a few more moments. Notice the beauty of peace within you. (Pause)

Now begin to focus your attention on your legs and your body while taking a big, deep breath—with the intention of returning your attention to the space of this room. When you are ready you can move voluntarily and open your eyes. Journaling your thoughts and insights can be very helpful.

How was that? Make a note in your journal and also keep in mind that the ideas shared near the end are a way to intentionally make changes in your performance and behavior. Back in 2001, I literally did what I just described as a way to sharpen my operating room skills when learning a new technique. I had an exceptionally low surgical complication rate with excellent outcomes, part of which I attribute to these types of mindful methods.

Now that you have some practical awareness of what it means to separate from your thoughts—that YOU are not your thoughts—let's explore some tools to better understand how thoughts and feelings determine your actions. This is the way to start recognizing the power of our storytelling brain to form the perceptions that are creating our "reality."

EXERCISE 2: THE POWER OF SELF-REFLECTION

We will need to learn self-reflection as adults. Our educational system discourages this, favoring over activity and too much "to do." When we are constantly thinking and doing too much, we feel overwhelmed, which triggers our stress response. This clouds our decision making and clarity. Typically, we will be less creative and empathetic as well. Learning how to be more self-reflective is an evolving discipline. Begin "small" and choose to incorporate some of the ideas from the following list into your daily routine. The more you do this, the easier it becomes; you can add other ideas as you grow.

Simple tools to exercise the Level 3 Brain, once meditation helps you to slow down:

- **Controlling Emotion**: Pause, count to six to break the tendency to react automatically before speaking.

- **Self-reflection**: What upsets me? Why do I feel this way? Why didn't I perform well today? Is this a pattern? How can I handle things differently next time? What do I *really* want? What inspires me?

- **Empathy**: What will inspire me to be more empathetic? What important relationship could it help? How will it help me to be a better leader? What can I do to have more self-acceptance and empathy? Why do I believe beating myself up is acceptable? Why do I believe it is okay to say harmful things to myself but not to other people? How would I feel if I were in their shoes? What are some reasons that the other person has for behaving this way? Can I listen and inquire instead of making assumptions?

- **Values**: What are my top five heart-felt values? How can I bring more of my values to my work and behavior?

- **Shift Your Body**: Take hourly stretch breaks; move around. This can help to short-circuit your survival brain and it feels good.

Staying too focused for too long creates mental and physical tension. It is well known that Albert Einstein and Thomas Edison took naps in the middle of the day, or took time to reflect, attributing a part of their genius to these rituals.

EXERCISE 3: MINDFULLY APPLIED MEANING
FOR EFFECTIVE COMMUNICATION

Recall from earlier chapters the following equation:

Thoughts + Emotion/Perception = Feelings => Actions

What we often do not realize is that this process is *subjective*. We could choose a different thought which would ultimately change our feelings and the actions taken. There is a **prevailing myth** that good decision making only comes from using our logical mind. Have you heard the saying, "Check your emotions at the front door when you come to the office"? This is another way of saying, "Check half of your human nature at the front door when you come to work." First of all, this is not realistic and no one is really doing it. Secondly, emotion is necessary and involved in effective decision making. In fact, research has shown that when the brain's hemispheres are surgically separated, people have trouble with very simple acts of decision-making, such as what clothes to wear. Can you imagine getting ready for work in the morning and being unable to decide what you will wear? And do you really think you will make major business decisions without the help of your emotional brain? Quite frankly, this myth and its attempted practice comes from a lack of brain and self-awareness.

Exercise three is meant to introduce the realization that our thought and emotions are constantly engaged in creating our life experiences. The more aware you are that you possess the power to choose your thoughts instead of only reacting to whatever comes to mind, the better a decision-maker and leader you will become. Realize that we are meaning-assigning beings. Our left-brain wants to understand what is going on. One important way to shift your experience and feelings is to change your perspective—your interpretation—of what you witness. When we are self-aware, we can use our left-brain to choose a different thought and meaning.

Again, this is a subjective process that is dependent on your attitudes, beliefs, and cellular memory about "how life is." In fact, if you believe that we are only victims of our thoughts and feelings, then you are not likely to take the initiative to do or understand this very exercise.

Compare the following scenarios describing an interaction between a manager who is thinking two different thoughts in response to her interpretation of the behavior of a person with whom she is engaged in conversation:

Scenario 1:

Thought: He doesn't want to listen to me; he's being disrespectful.

Emotion/Perception: Fear (move away)

Feeling: Anger, frustration, insecurity

Action: Raise your voice, act defensively, or shut down
the conversation

Now, with pausing, reframing, and from a perspective of keeping an open, empathetic mind (which takes self-awareness and self-confidence), consider the response to the same situation in Scenario 2.

Scenario 2:

Thought: Perhaps I do not understand him or I am not making myself clear; let me inquire.

Emotion/Perception: Love (move toward)

Feeling: Calm, relaxed, patient

Action: Inquire into what the other person is thinking and feeling; seek to understand. Ask questions to reflect how the person perceived what was said and consider ways to reframe the words or context. As a leader, you respond with the willingness to understand others instead of defensively assuming you know what they are thinking.

The way a person thinks and feels is how they "show up" in the world. We can pretend only so long and even then, other people are often intuitive enough to see through the false pretense. When we are self-aware of our own thoughts, emotion, and feelings, we are better able to self-manage (an emotional intelligence competency) and make wise, productive choices. We can "show up" authentically, matching our words to our feelings, and naturally taking action from this congruent space. This concept is powerful because our thoughts, feelings, and actions are the ingredients that go into creating our life experience.

For this exercise, reflect on some recent conversations you have had that contained conflict and did not result ideally or as you intended. Take journal notes using this process of remembering what you thought in the midst of the situation, and record your perception or emotional response, how it made you feel, and what you did. Then re-imagine the same situation, but this time think a thought that is more empathetic or curious instead of "already knowing" the other's intent or automatically defending yourself. How did changing your thought evolve the whole equation and theoretically provide a different outcome? How does it feel in your body? Why not venture out to revisit the person again, coming from your new place of self-awareness, and see if this can change the relationship dynamic in a positive way?

EXERCISE 4—YOUR IDEAL SELF

"Ideal self" is a commonly used term, the origin of which is not clear. Another term is "Ideal Future Self." When I was in training for my coaching certification, we were taught NLP techniques (neuro-linguistic programming) which use the term, "future self." This is a method for creating your future experience with more intention and clarity. We use the technique I described above, "Visioning by Design," which first involves getting clear about the desired behaviors and attitudes of your future self before relaxing into the mindfulness practice. While relaxed, you create the future image of what you want, and feel the accompanying feelings in order to align with the images created in your mind's eye. *We create images in our mind all the time; commonly, they are images that we don't want.* In order for the brain to believe your mental movie, you must also use as much sensory input as possible, such as hearing, seeing others who would be involved in general terms, incorporating the details of texture and touch if possible.

I previously discussed the difference between the ego (personality) mental concept self that is formed from autobiographical cellular memory and the True Self. Your True Self is your spirit self that animates your physical body. Some people may think of this as "conscious awareness"—your "self" without labels, judgments and social conditionings that make up the ego. It can also be thought of as our authentic self or heart and soul. This part of you is the source of your true potential and life purpose. We tend not to give much time to understanding our inner self, so the vocabulary is not well defined in general. You can think of your ego as your "current personality self" or your current self-identity. It is how you present yourself to the external world around you. Remember that our personality "self" (the ego) is ever-evolving. When we are aware of how our brain and mind work, we can create a more functional, "future personality self" on purpose (a more functional ego construct). This is a way of transforming your ego mental construct of yourself, which leads to a change in your perception and subsequent behavior patterns. Where we are at this moment can shift tomorrow; that is what revelation and transformation is all about. Our personality is not written in stone. We can change our behavior and how we see our self (our self-image). The deeper we come to know and understand our True Self, the more likely we are to align with our core values and live a fulfilling life. The exercise in this section is meant to help you begin to understand with greater clarity how to accelerate the process of personal transformation. We can proactively use our brains to change our current self-identity "narrative" in a way that aligns with our hearts and souls so that we can live more fulfilling and productive lives. Re-inventing your narrative about your current identity requires awareness of how the brain creates our self-identity, (discussed in chapter five), then using exercises to apply this information pragmatically.

Our current identity is based on past narrative assumptions and current mindset. If we don't reflect on our past story as it surfaces, attempting to reframe it with feeling and with big-picture context and compassion, we will continue to bring this narrative into our present moment. We must get clear about our intention/motive, define what character virtues we'd like to incorporate into our lives, connect this with our purpose, and then write a new script for the future in order to rewire our brains. A prerequisite is our willingness to let go of "victim consciousness" and blame in order to make this work—"victim" conflicts with "victor." This concept can help you develop new skill sets, engage behavior modification, attain new roles or life experiences in general, even see yourself your ideal way within the context of your relationships. Your mind and subconscious is listening to your narrative! You may as well write the script constructively instead of destructively. The underlying concept is that you are giving your mind a new template for what you desire to manifest in the physical world—especially important since, your brain and mind are amazing at producing "self-fulfilling prophecy." Just remember that you must feel it as well as see it. Feeling is an ingredient for belief and thus experience. Remember these points:

1. Focusing on where you are reinforces that signal to your brain. If you think of yourself as unchangeable, you will

engage a self-fulfilling prophecy and you will, of course, stay stuck!

2. Our brain works through focused attention. If we keep talking about the current circumstance and feeling the same way, we will keep doing the same things. Essentially, we strengthen the wires in our brain, which is the basis of habit formation.

3. In order to break your focused attention, you must give your brain a "new vision." This is necessary to begin to "expand your vision." You must see it in your mind's eye. That is the premise of creating your "ideal future self." You have to "see it to believe it."

In reality, things have always worked in this fashion. The identity that we "believe" about ourselves ultimately shows up, and the longer and stronger we believe, the more challenging it becomes to change it. Visioning by design is the way out. Albert Einstein held this same premise:

Your imagination is your preview to life's coming attractions.

It is important to remember that it's not just about seeing the vision; you must feel it as well. Feelings are the juice of creation. Passion pulls you forward. Positive emotion makes us happier, healthier, and more energetic. We perform better and stay more focused and efficient. There needs to be a big-picture meaning—a "Why"—for reaching the future self. The more purposeful and noble your goal, the more likely you will be sustainably happy, even in the face of challenge. Many people retreat from their vision because their hearts are not into it. Heart delivers courage, wisdom, perseverance, and values. It is what connects you to people and making a difference. A short-term focus, having only a "me" orientation of acquiring material things without a noble purpose, makes life transactional and ultimately empty. Yet, when we pursue our purpose and then acquire wealth, it is like frosting on the cake; it can be enjoyed, but is not the main dish.

Because of society's focus on negative emotion and worry, most people are carrying a negative polarity of feelings within their minds and bodies. Passion and joy, which are both considered positive feelings in our language, are buried underneath. On the way to finding them, you are most likely going to hit some old wounds and bumps. There are a variety of methods to release these old feelings. These range from "sitting" with them as they rage about, to using visualization practices to move them up and out. There is even a process known as "tapping" on the body's energy meridians (also known as EFT or Emotional Freedom Technique), which facilitates easier release of trapped feelings from the body's cellular memory. Though I will not go into greater detail about this particular process, it is important to recognize that the more you become mindful and quiet your mind through meditation, the better prepared you will be to take the next steps and "make friends with feelings." Calming of emotion is a side effect of regular mindfulness practice. My intent is to support you as you begin to change your intention and perception about the nature and importance of feelings. Until you become self-aware of these ideas, you have little to no hope of becoming skillful at self-management of your feelings.

For exercise 4, make a list with two columns, one to list your current personality traits and one to list the roles you play. These are the essentials of how you define your self-identity. Personality traits will begin with the words, "I am _____" and roles typically are defined as, "I am a/an _____." You want to do this in order to describe your current self and how you desire to evolve your future self. For example, "I am disciplined" would be a personality trait. "I am a physician" would be a role.

This exercise is a basic technique to help you become aware of your current starting point and become acquainted with yourself. So many people are too busy to slow down in order to see themselves where they currently are in any real depth. Also, we tend to overlook our assets and focus too much on our "weaknesses." Balance is achieved by keeping a holistic approach. In order to begin, choose ten personality traits and ten roles that are at the very top of your list when describing yourself:

Current Self:

Personality Trait (I am _____)	Role (I am a/an _____)
1.	
2.	
3.	
4.	
5.	
6.	
7.	
8.	
9.	
10.	

It is important to distinguish traits and roles because what you put behind "I am_____" will begin to create your state of being over time, especially when identifying traits and roles with feeling. Also, it is important to begin realizing how we confuse who we are with what we do. If we think we are our roles, who are we when we leave those roles? Who you are is not what you do. This type of exercise is meant to help you become conscious of the difference. You can become more observant of your roles as separate from your sense of Self.

Before you create your Ideal self, it would be optimal to have reflected on your values, your purpose, and, if you have one, a mission. Having a clear and definite purpose keeps us from being distracted constantly by the environment and supports the likelihood that we will achieve our dreams and goals. Also, always include your "why" for wanting any goal. The "why" fuels your passion; the nobler the reason for your goal, the more likely your heart will engage it as well.

Another exercise I like to offer is taking the time to reflect on current assets, balanced by where you have room for growth opportunities (weaknesses). Determining this type of balance sheet list is a good time to reflect on your "should's" and "ought to's" so that you can sweep them clear from the clutter in your mind. If you are telling yourself "you need to learn something," but there is no intuitive or gut heart feeling that it is something your authentic self aspires to do, simply delegate it. Creative, truly successful people do not attempt to do everything. They know who they are, and they build upon their heart's desires, talents, and purpose instead of micro-managing their worlds. Engage support and allow others to shine at what they are good at doing.

In summary, reflection time is time well spent, and we must learn how to incorporate it into our behavior. If you do not have time to reflect now, what makes you think you will have more time when you need to begin again, or when you realize that your intended destination is not what you want? We waste time, energy, and money because we are not clear. We never live fulfilling lives because we don't know who we are or what we really want. The habit of reflection can stop your drifting so that you can develop a clear and definite purpose. Our brains and minds need a clear target or else we will drift through life.

Once you have completed the above exercise, reflect on what personality traits you would like to have in your leadership role and your life, as well as what roles would be congruent with your authentic self. As a leader, what roles would you like to specifically play, e.g., mentor, coach, or how would you like to communicate your vision (a narrative or story that paints a *mental image*) to your team and organization? Are you an extroverted leader? Are you an introverted leader? Your personality will influence your choice of roles. Also, to the degree that you have mapped out your values, purpose, and meaning, you will feel more passion and enthusiasm instead of simply going through the motions of this exercise.

Ideal Future Self:

Personality Trait (I am _____)	Role (I am a/an _____)
1.	
2.	
3.	
4.	
5.	
6.	
7.	
8.	
9.	
10.	

Now, take this list into your mindfulness space and begin to envision as much detail as possible about situations involving others, where you can enact your new "future self" traits and roles. ***See and feel now*** because <u>now</u> (your body can only be in the present moment) is the only time that you can rewire and retrain your brain. Repeat this mindfulness meditation as often as you can, even if for only minutes at a time. Tweak your mental movie as you go and as new ideas and "ahas" come through. This is a basic introduction to the idea of taking back control of our own thoughts, feelings, and the trajectory for our lives—by creating on purpose.

EXERCISE 5: CALLING IT OUT—NAME IT AND RETRAIN IT

I am going to make a short digression here to highlight a point that I think is important to "Transcending Limiting Mindsets," which I refer to in the sub-title of this book. Many years ago, I became terrified of feeling and I had a very boisterous "inner critic." I had been living too much "in my head," and I was shutting down and guarding, or really *imprisoning* my heart. As I determined to free my mind from this intellectual tyranny, I went through many trials and errors. One day I noticed a pattern and asked myself, "What if instead of running away by repressing the mental chatter or staying busy so that I could divert my attention, I began to "call it out"—to call out my thought, sometimes verbally?" I noticed that the chatter would dissipate if I named it and spoke it aloud, verbally announcing, "There's that thought; I won't receive it" and then switched to a positive affirmation. Or I would name the negative feeling that was provoking my angst and declared that instead I felt a self-directed positive feeling (even though frankly I didn't really necessarily feel it strongly or at all at the time). The negative feeling would also dissipate as I did this.

Once I became aware of this effect, I persisted and began to notice less frequent mind chatter. There were other strategies that I also used to stop the negative self-talk habit, but this one seemed particularly effective. I came to call this exercise "Calling it Out," and I taught it to others this way.

Fast forward. Neuroscience started producing results from clinical studies demonstrating that this process of naming the negative thought and feeling intentionally quieted the fight/flight stress response. It was like shining a light into a dark space. Remember how as a child, if you actually looked under that bed instead of running away, you discovered that there was really nothing to be afraid of—that there was no boogeyman hiding under the bed? Calling it out had that same feeling of freedom from fear. What I did not realize at the time was that I was literally rewiring and retraining my brain by changing my response. I just knew it was working. While this is a pointed example of how science can help us to become more consciously aware of what is going on within us physiologically, I am not an advocate for waiting on science or some other outside authority to supersede your own intuitive voice. I have extensive background training in science; yet my motto is, "Be informed, but not intimated" by science. Science has its own limitations; if we want to reach our true potential, we must learn to trust our own inner knowing and truth without needing permission to do so. *Think for yourself.*

Fortunately, I had the courage to trust my empirical experience and hence I had a head start on science by way of experiential application. Since research validates that we can rewire and retrain our brains, I now use the phrase, "Name it and Retrain It" instead of the phrase "calling it out" because this more accurately and completely describes the process. Transcending limiting mindsets will require at times that you have the courage to move ahead of the crowd. This is what innovation requires; if it exists within the known world, it is already old news.

Both brain hemispheres form autobiographical memory. Our emotional and right brains hold the feelings and memory in place with a contextual meaning that the left-brain has assigned. The left-brain plays an important role in directing the narrative of the story. It directs the trajectory of the perception created, while the emotional and right-brain receives the conscious mind sensory input (meaning assignment also) and stores it accordingly. The memory is stored according to the meaning, feelings and context ascribed to it at the time of the event. This is a subjective process, which explains why various people can have totally different memories of the same event.

Split-brain studies have demonstrated how the left-brain is adept at "making up meaning," even if this does not reflect accurate factual evidence. So the best way to change autobiographical memory is to intentionally engage the cooperation of the left-brain because it has a lot of impact on the feeling response. The left-brain is uncomfortable with feelings. If engaged, it will be less likely to stimulate the stress response. Once the left-brain is proactively engaged, old scary memories and feelings can come to light without so much emotional drama. Naming our thought or feeling engages the left-brain. We can more easily access outdated subconscious thoughts and feelings when we are self-aware and recognize the need for our left-brain to name what is going on within us. We can then make a conscious choice with a positive affirmation to re-direct our attention and begin to retrain our brain. Remember that an affirmation spoken out loud is engaging the left verbal brain by definition. It is our left-brain that gives us the ability to speak. We can then, with intention, direct our attention to the right brain's expertise for envisioning new mental images and accessing positive feelings such as compassion and gratitude on purpose, *with purpose*. We can use our right-brain, which thinks in pictures, to expand our vision for a new response. Hence, Name it and Retrain It is a collaborative effort between both brain hemispheres to create a new autobiographical narrative.

Research with obsessive-compulsive disorder (OCD), a much more severe form of "self-talk," has revealed that when patients learned meditation to calm their minds and separate their sense of self from their thoughts, it helped them to switch their compulsive thinking. When they named the anxiety-producing thought or feeling and switched their attention to a positive pre-planned affirmation, their stress and anxiety decreased. In fact, their brain's "worry circuits" actually decreased over time, even to normal parameters. When practiced consistently, this affect occurred in a matter of weeks. This also powerfully illustrates neuroplasiticity and how quickly our brains can literally rewire when we are persistent and disciplined in our approach. Here are the steps in order:

1. Fear-provoking thought stimulus becomes conscious.

2. Name it; call it out—"There's that OCD thought," for example.

3. Switch the thought verbally if possible, to a prepared positive affirmation such as, "I am growing calmer and more self-aware every day." Keep repeating positive phrases that occupy your mind instead of indulging negative thinking. Your mind will not be able to occupy two opposing thoughts simultaneously.

It is also useful to intentionally pause and see in your mind's eye (imagination) a new, premeditated constructed behavior, which is your Ideal Self response. See yourself acting in your mind's eye in the most optimal way you can imagine, as you state your desired outcomes with your affirmations. There are ways to anchor positive feelings of gratitude to these mental images that powerfully support the affirmations. I have found some truth in the adage, "act grateful and you will be grateful." Also, this will change your "vibe" in that you will find you attract more to be grateful for. It's interesting how repeating the statement "I am grateful," along with the intention to feel so, tends to create the feeling of gratitude with consistent practice. With or without the support of science, I know it works for me. I will therefore continue using these ideas to bring positive transformation into my life experience.

I began to combine the method of "calling it out" with creating my future self back in 2001. I used the "theater of the mind" with intention to hone my surgical skill. I had taken a short sabbatical from surgery, and I was feeling nervous about going back into the operating room. I was also feeling pressure to update my technique at the same time. I set a goal to refine my cataract surgery technique to what is known as "clear cornea," which means to do cataract surgery with such a small wound incision so that sutures are not required to close the wound.

Fortunately, I had become self-aware enough to hear and recognize the voice of fear in my mind, and I knew I had to stop it or it would only escalate. I followed naming the negative thought with not only affirmations, but I also created an intentional mental movie. I imagined not only the technique but also doing it very quickly and calmly. It involved seeing it in my mind's eye (image), creating a positive affirmation script, and feeling gratitude. I did this while in a relaxed, mindful state of mind, which improves learning and integration. (I now recognize this concept as, "Name it and Retrain It.") This idea of mental rehearsal to develop our skill is an old idea that professional athletes have used for some time. Its application can be used in all areas of our personal and professional lives. It works for me, and I have received wonderful feedback from clients who have begun to use these applications of neuroscience in a practical way.

RESILIENCY AS A LIFESTYLE: INTEGRATION

Mind has an emotional and intellectual component. A whole brain creates the experience of a whole life. This journey of personal and professional growth is a marathon, not a quick-fix, short sprint. The more self-aware and committed we become, the less time will be required. Patience really is a virtue. Integration begins within, and as people make this personal commitment, many of the silos we see all around us will dissolve. Before we can effectively collaborate with others, we must be able to engage our brain hemispheres in a collaborative relationship. Peace begins within you as well. Resiliency develops out of challenge. Will you rise to the occasion? These are times for great opportunity or great disappointment. How you see it will depend on your perception of it; your vision directs the path to your ultimate destination. Where will you go from here? It is my hope that you too will choose to transcend a limiting mindset to become a more engaging leader. I sincerely hope you join me. I truly hope you choose to, Be YOU, *Magnificently.*

Key Points

- If we wish to expand the vision for our lives, we need to apply the knowledge that we learn in our everyday life. This is not a quick fix, one-day event. It is a practice that takes practice.

- Holistically cultivating the four levels of your human self intentionally—on purpose—spiritually, emotionally, mentally and physically—is necessary for sustainable personal transformation and change.

- The take-home for mindfulness meditation is rooted in the principle that the mind is most efficient when learning in a state of calm presence, and open curiosity, instead of "already knowing that" or feeling anxious.

- We must begin to increase our self-awareness as leaders and tap more of the qualities of the right-brain hemisphere and Level 3 Thrival brain, such as greater emotional intelligence skills, self-management of feelings, and ways to expand our innovative and creative capacities.

- Meditation is also central to reducing stress, which is now an epidemic and very damaging to our physical, cognitive, and social/emotional health.

- You can also imagine and create a more expanded vision for your life, once you develop the mind muscle of your Level 3 brain. This is how I want you to understand the tool of mindfulness; it is foundational to brain integration, making change easier and more lasting.

- To slow down your brain waves doesn't make you less ambitious or lazy. There is a myth that being mindful means losing one's drive or motivation for performance or success.

- Our educational system discourages self-reflection in favor of over-activity and too much "to do." When we constantly think and do too much, we feel overwhelmed, and this triggers our stress response.

- There is a **prevailing myth** that good decision-making only comes from using our logical mind.

- Emotion is necessary and involved in effective decision-making.

- Remember that our "self" is multi-dimensional and is ever-evolving. Where we are at this moment can shift tomorrow; that is what revelation and transformation is all about.

- Our current identity is based on past narrative assumptions and current mindset.

- We must get clear about our intention/motive, define what character virtues we would like to incorporate into our lives, connect these with our purpose, and then write a new script for the future in order to rewire our brains.

- Split-brain studies demonstrate that the left-brain is adept at "making up meaning," even if this does not reflect accurate factual evidence. Thus, the best way to change autobiographical memory is to intentionally engage the left-brain to cooperate.

- Naming our thought or feeling engages the left-brain.

- A whole brain creates the experience of a whole life.

Reflection: Inquiring Mind

1. What has been your track record for staying on a personal growth and transformation course? Do you tend to need more accountability instead of going it alone? If you need

more accountability, what are your thoughts about receiving coaching support?

2. How has understanding the "operating system" of your brain helped you to make sense of your life's journey to this point?

3. What benefits can you see from clarifying your dreams and goals before charging off toward your next goal?

4. How can you incorporate the lessons of this book into your leadership development plan?

5. How can you incorporate the lessons of this book into helping your team develop their strengths and improve their performance and engagement?

Envision Possibilities

1. What does an active learning training curriculum look like? How would it actually help team members own and apply new professional development? Imagine how much more willing people would be to learn if they knew the process allowed them to live with greater purpose and happiness, at work and at home.

2. Can you imagine creating a program that integrates adult learning into the everyday workplace experience?

3. How different would your current workplace look and feel if people were truly productive and engaged? Imagine a place where people loved coming to work.

EPILOGUE

We are being "called" to know our self; our current state of business affairs and personal trials are simply magnifying the urgency of the need to cultivate this new understanding. This self-knowing is the core of a healthy root system for growing all other leadership competencies. It is the foundation of sustainable personal growth and development. Until we first turn our attention inward to develop the self-awareness and "intrapersonal" skills for authenticity and a curious and open-mind, we will neither reach the true potential of our personal or professional self nor the true potential of our organizations. It is imperative that we learn how to integrate our spirit, emotion, mind, and body within our self—within our mind and heart—if we are to integrate and eliminate the silos that are wrecking our organizations and social institutions.

Our modern times hold opportunities to learn how to cultivate the "seed of opportunity" to be found within the adversities that seem to intermittently spring up around us during various periods of our lives. While adversity is excessively intense for many at this time, due to economic and social turmoil around the world, it won't be the last time we will face challenging experiences of change. My own life early on seemed to be filled with adversity, disappointment, and the lack of external guidance and support. While it was difficult and uncomfortable at the time, I can see now how I was potentially being prepared for "such a time as this." I had to learn how to turn inward to look for answers because I was not seeing my way clear to the destinations I desired. I also had to come face to face with a host of fears, self-doubt, and ways of seeing life that was myopic and constrictive. It is little wonder to me why I so highly value the power of vision. It saved me from wrecking my life and wasting my potential.

I can say, without reservation, that it was my inner courage and willingness to make the necessary inner journey to take back control of the "steering wheel of my mind" and think beyond the limitations placed before me that ultimately made all the difference. I had to question my own limited beliefs about myself, others, and the world at large. In so doing, I began to gain the insights I needed to "restore my vision" and "free my mind." I now have the mindset and tools to live a resiliently productive, fulfilling, and peace-filled life as well as to contribute in valuable ways to the lives of others. It has been worth the effort and as I look back, I could not be who I am today without the adversity that I faced, engaged in, and evolved through.

It is my hope that the information and tips shared in this book, which is an introduction to a new paradigm of living and leadership, will help to shorten your learning curve and make your journey less intimidating than mine was for me. Now that we have the neuroscience, a social and business context of urgency to deal with the adversity we face, and are living in a time where people are searching for new answers, we can more openly and collaboratively move ourselves forward into this new frontier of personal and professional growth and development. I have faith in the inner genius of humanity and I intend to keep that faith as we move forward and upward to the heights of purposeful leadership and creative potential. I wish you the courage it takes to change and grow so that you can experience great success in all that you undertake and with all you believe in, especially your SELF.

Anchor, S. (2010). *The happiness advantage: Seven principles of positive psychology that fuel success and performance at work.* New York, NY: Crown Business.

Benson, H. (1975/2000). *The relaxation response.* New York, NY: Harper-Torch, An Imprint of HarperCollins Publishers.

Bolte-Taylor, J. (2006). *My stroke of insight: A brain scientist's personal journey.* New York, NY: Penguin Group USA.

Budworth, M., & Mann, S. L. (2010). Becoming a leader: The challenge of modesty for women. *Journal of Management Development, 29*(2), 177–186.

Collins, J. (2001). *Good to great: Why some companies make the leap...and some don't.* New York, NY: HarperCollins Publishers.

Conant, D. (2011, October 13). Keeping employees engaged in tough times [Blog podcast]. Retrieved from http://blogs.hbr.org/ideacast/2011/10/keeping-employees-engaged-in-t.html

Coontz, S. (2011). *A strange stirring: The feminine mystique and American women at the dawn of the 1960s.* New York, NY: Basic Books.

Davidson, R. J., & Begley, S. (2010). *The emotional life of your brain: How its unique patterns affect the way you think, feel, and live—and how you can change them.* New York, NY: Hudson Street Press.

Derntl, B., Finkelmeyer, A., Eickhoff, S., Kellerman, T., Falkenberg, D. I., Schneider, F., & Habel, U. (2010, January). Multidimensional assessment of empathic abilities. *Psychoneuroendocrinology Journal, 35*(1), 67–82.

Eagly, A. H., & Karau, S. J. (2002). Role congruity theory of prejudice toward female leaders. *Psychological Review, 109,* 573–598. doi:10.1037/0033-295X.109.3.573

Eichhorn, N. (2012, Spring). Safety: The preamble for social engagement, an interview with Stephen W. Poges, PhD. *Somatic Psychotherapy Today, 1*(4).

Eliot, L. (2009). *Pink brain, blue brain: How small differences grow into troublesome gaps—and what we can do about it.* Boston, MA: Houghton Mifflin Harcourt.

Friedman, C. K., Leaper, C., & Bigler, R. S. (2007). Do mother's gender related attitudes or comments predict young children's gender beliefs? *Parenting: Science and Practice, 7*(4), 1–10.

George, B. (2012, February 17). A new era for global leadership development. *Harvard Business Review.* Retrieved from http://www.billgeorge.org/page/global-leadership-series

Goleman, D., Boyatzis, R., & McKee, A. (2002). *Primal leadership: Learning to lead with emotional intelligence.* Boston, MA: Harvard Business School Press.

Jordon-Young, R. M. (2010). *Brainstorm: The flaws in the science of sex differences.* Cambridge, MA: Harvard University Press.

Kotter, J. P. (1996). *Leading change.* Boston, MA: Harvard Business Press.

Lee, H. (2011). Understanding the battle of the sexes: The effect of gender on leadership style. Barrett Values Centre. Retrieved from http://www.valuescentre.com/resources/?sec=articles

Lopez Torregrosa, L. (2010, July 24). On Wall St., Gender bias runs deep [Interview with Ilene H. Lang, *The New York Times*]. Retrieved from http://www.nytimes.com/2012/07/25/us/25iht-letter25.html

Maslow, A. H. (1943). A theory of human motivation. *Psychological Review, 50*(4), 370–396. Retrieved from http://psychclassics.yorku.ca/Maslow/motivation.htm

McGilchrist, I. (2012). *The master and his emissary: The divided brain and the making of the Western world.* London, UK: Yale University Press.

Michalaka, K. J., Kinzler, K. D., & Decety, J. (2012). Age-related sex differences in explicit measures of empathy do not predict brain responses across childhood and adolescence. *Developmental Cognitive Neuroscience Journal, 3,* 22–32.

Myatt, M. (2012, December 12). 10 reasons your top talent will leave you. *Forbes.* http://www.forbes.com/sites/mikemyatt/2012/12/13/10-reasons-your-top-talent-will-leave-you

Nash, A., & Grossi, G. (2007). Picking Barbie™'s brain: Inherent sex differences in scientific ability? *Journal of Interdisciplinary Feminist Thought* 2(1), 29–42. Retrieved from http://digitalcommons.salve.edu/jift/vol2/iss1/5/

Pascual-Leone, A., Amedi, A., Fregni, F., & Merabet, L. B. (2005, July). The plastic human brain cortex. *Annual Review of Neuroscience, 28,* 377–401.

Pink, D. H. (2009). *Drive: The surprising truth about what motivates us.* New York, NY: Riverhead Books.

Powell, C. (2012). *It worked for me: In life and leadership.* New York, NY: HarperCollins Publishers.

Rosener, J. B. (1990, November-December). Ways women lead. *Harvard Business Review, 68*(6), 119–125. Retrieved from http://hbr.org/1990/11/ways-women-lead/ar/

Sandberg, S. (2013). *Lean in: Women, work, and the will to lead.* New York, NY: Alfred A. Knopf.

Siegel, D. J. (2010). *Mindsight: The new science of personal transformation.* New York, NY: Bantam Books.

Thompson, J. (1999). *Alpha relaxation system: Soothe your body, calm your mind, enhance your health* [Audio CD]. New York, NY: The Relaxation Company.

Thompson, J. (1999). *Theta meditation system: Let go of stress, renew your spirit, gain insight and intuition* [Audio CD]. New York, NY: The Relaxation Company.

Wittenberg-Cox, A. (2010). *How women mean business: A step by step guide to profiting from gender balanced business.* Chichester, UK: John Wiley & Sons Ltd.

Zenger, J., & Folkman, J. (2012, March 15). Are women better leaders than men? [HBR Blog Network]. Retrieved from http://blogs.hbr.org/cs/2012/03/a_study_in_leadership_women_do.html

Valencia Ray, M.D.

Before selling her medical practice, Valencia Ray, M.D., was a practicing eye surgeon for over two decades. Taking her life purpose of *"restoring vision"* to a new level, she now helps corporate and entrepreneurial leaders, and other professionals expand their vision for their lives. Using The Art and Science of **NeuroReInvention®** (NRI), she helps these professionals—regardless of gender—tap into the secret of sustainable, dynamic leadership, performance, and well-being.

For ongoing tips, tools and strategies to access your true potential and perform at your best, visit www.ValenciaRay.com.

Made in the USA
Monee, IL
31 July 2021